THE
YEAR
I WAS
BORN

Compiled by Alison Graham

Signpost Books

Published by Signpost Books, Ltd
25 Eden Drive, Headington, Oxford OX3 0AB

First published 1995
10 9 8 7 6 5 4 3 2 1

Based on an original idea by Sally Wood
Conceived, designed and produced by Signpost Books, Ltd
Copyright in this format © Signpost Books, Ltd 1995
Compiler: Alison Graham
Designer: Paul Fry
Editor: Dorothy Wood

ISBN 1 874785 23 6

Acknowledgments: Mirror Group Newspapers plc. for all the pictures in which they hold
copyright, and Hugh Gallacher for his invaluable help in retrieving them from the files; Associated
Press, pp. 4, 20 and back cover, 35, 44, 60, 72, 80-81; Hulton-Deutsch Collection, pp. 10, 19, 30, 33,
42, 77, 93; Popperfoto, pp. 12-13, 44; PA News, p. 80; Topham, pp. 53, 58-59, 65.
Every effort has been made to trace all copyright holders, but if any have been inadvertently
overlooked, the publishers will be pleased to make the necessary arrangements at the first opportunity.

Printed and bound in Italy.

Front cover pictures: (clockwise, from top): King George V's funeral; Amy Mollison;
Jesse Owens, Jarrow marchers, King Edward VIII and Wallis Simpson (the Duke and Duchess
of Windsor).

ME THEN

ME NOW

PERSONAL PROFILE

Names:

Date of Birth:

Place of Birth: **Time of Birth:**

Weight at Birth: **Parents' names:**

Colour of Eyes: **Colour of Hair:**

Distinguishing Marks: **Weight now:**

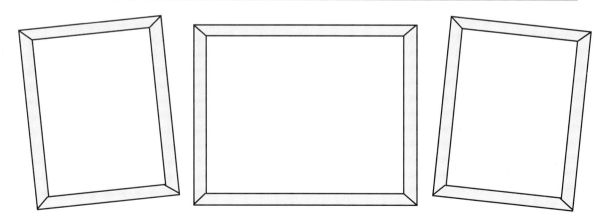

MY FAMILY

1 Wednesday
New Year's Day

A law **banning Jews** from employing women under the age of 35 comes into force in Germany. 10,000 women lose their jobs.

■ The first Transatlantic solo flyer Col Charles Lindbergh arrives in Liverpool with his wife and baby boy, Jon. **The Lindberghs**, *left,* want to get away from America following the kidnapping and murder of their five-year-old son last year.

. . . Concert pianist Myra Hess and Christabel Pankhurst, champion of the votes for women campaign, become DBEs in the New Year's Honours list . . .

■ Merchant navy officers form a **trades union** — Navigators and Engineer Officers Union — to demand a pay increase of 25%, a month's paid leave p.a., a contributory pension scheme, and recognised work hours.

■ A **rail plane** invented by George Rennie capable of travelling at 100mph, could link Central London to Croydon Airport on a track built over the southern railway line from Holborn Viaduct to Croydon. It has already been successful in Glasgow.

2 Thursday

The River **Thames bursts** its banks at Maidenhead. There is widespread flooding in the Home Counties, Kent and Bedfordshire.

■ The *New York Daily Post* calls Col Lindbergh the 'Greta Garbo of the Air' for leaving the USA.

■ News arrives of an Imperial Airways flying boat which crashed outside Alexandria, Egypt, on New Year's Eve, killing 12. There is only one survivor.

. . . HITLER tells the League of Nations not to interfere in Germany's treatment of its Jewish population . . .

3 Friday

Desperate last-minute efforts are being made to save **Bruno Hauptmann,** convicted murderer of the Lindbergh baby, who is due to be executed at 8am on January 14.

■ The Polish government in Warsaw frees 27,000 **prisoners** under a general amnesty.

■ Tommy Tuohy, the last of the Six Terrible Brothers who led Chicago's gang of kidnappers, racketeers and jewel thieves, has been captured by police after a two-and-a-half year search. He was called the **Human Bomb** because he kept a phial of explosives in his pocket. His gang was 100 strong and they travelled in armoured cars.

4 Saturday

The Prince of Wales is among the crowd at Twickenham to see **Alexander Obolensky** (19), *below,* the Russian prince who came to England as a baby and is now at Oxford, score two tries in the international against New Zealand. England beat the All-Blacks for the first time, 13-0.

. . . The first HIT PARADE appears in the magazine Billboard in New York . . .

5 Sunday

Storms lash Britain, with gusts reaching 85mph. New York is ice and snow bound.

■ Italy will not participate in the **Davis Cup** this year because of League of Nations sanctions against her over Abyssinia.

■ It is reported that the actress **Edith Evans** has become so keen on ice skating that she is cutting morning rehearsals of John Gielgud's *Romeo and Juliet.*

6 Monday

■ The Cunard White Star liner *Scythia* is taken over by the War Department as a **troop ship** — the first time for many years an Atlantic liner has been chartered by the government.

■ News from the **January Sales**: Marshall & Snelgrove: Natural

Hogskin gloves, 7s.11d; Swan & Edgar: Lace cami-knickers, 2s.11d; Squirrel cape, 7gns.; Spun Celanese vests , 2s. Galeries Lafayette: wool jumpers, 3s.6d; Wool frocks, 7s.11d.

7 Tuesday

Provincetown, Massachusetts, sends a letter to Col Lindbergh offering him refuge. It has not had a single crime since its foundation in 1727.

■ The **execution** of **Bruno Hauptmann**, *right,* is delayed until January 17 so that his appeal to have his sentence commuted to life imprisonment can be heard.

■ Threat of **floods** in Paris as the Seine rises to an alarming level. The Grand Canal in Dublin overflows, driving 50 people from their homes.

. . . A COW ESCAPES from its drover in Bristol causing havoc in the streets. It wrecks a tobacconist's shop and a draper's and scatters hundreds of women shoppers on its two-mile rampage through the centre of the city before it is cornered . . .

8 Wednesday
Full moon

German girls must be hardened with Spartan severity, says an article in *Arbeitsmann,* the organ of the German Labour Service. They must accustom themselves to the straw pallet, renounce all artificial aids to beauty, wear only simple uniform clothing and abstain from all pleasure and delicacies.

. . . Two Air France flying boats, carrying mail for South America, pass and salute each other in mid-Atlantic for the first time, at an estimated speed of 300mph. . .

■ The MCC recommend that the experimental LBW rule should be adopted in all cricket played in Great Britain.

BIG DEAL: West Ham sign Dartford's Fred Dell (20) for a fee of £1,250—the highest sum ever paid for a player without experience in the Football League.

. . . There is a TOTAL ECLIPSE of the sun today, visible from Greenwich . . .

9 Thursday

The US Democratic party endorses **Franklin D Roosevelt** as its candidate for the 1936 Presidential election.

■ Vickers reveal that its new anti-aircraft gun is being bought by all the foreign powers, but not one has been ordered by Britain, whose present AA guns date back to 1918.

. . . The 10,000th HILLMAN MINX comes off the production line . . .

■ France moves its 1st and 2nd squadrons (more than 70 ships) to the Mediterranean, to be in place when the League of Nations considers a possible oil **embargo** on Italy.

■ Dr F M H Taylor tells the Institution of Heating Engineers that he can visualize a time when **hot water** and heating are automatically altered to a lower temperature at night.

. . . JOHN GILBERT, *right,* **the screen's perfect lover, dies of heart failure aged 38 . . .**

10 Friday

100mph gales sweep England.

■ Mrs Miles, the mother of the St Neots quads, born just before Christmas, is allowed to help feed her babies for the first time . . .

■ Spectators at the **Olympic Games** in Berlin in August will be supplied with waterproof raincoats made of oiled paper and costing a 1¾ d each, in case of bad weather.

11 Saturday

200 miners at the Ynyscedwyn pit start a stay-down **strike** in protest against heavy

damages claimed against them by the company for alleged infringements of the Mines Act.

... It is reported that the RAF is set to expand at the rate of a squadron a week ...

■ The first folio edition of Shakespeare's plays—the Lefferts Copy—fetches $28,000 at auction in New York.

12 Sunday

General Goering celebrates his 43rd birthday in Berlin with a ball at the State Opera House. There are 2,100 guests, most of whom pay £4 a ticket. Everyone, including nearly every ambassador, is there — except Hitler and Goebbels.

13 Monday

Author and poet Rudyard Kipling undergoes surgery at the Middlesex Hospital, London, for a gastric complaint.

■ Divorce rate rises. There were 3,934 divorces in 1935.

... Bruno Hauptmann's appeal against execution fails ...

■ Devon is covered in 18ins of snow.

14 Tuesday

Mrs Marjorie Barbirolli is granted a decree for the restitution of conjugal rights in the divorce court against her husband, famous conductor **Giovanni (John) Barbirolli,** *left.*

■ Salary Scale 1 for elementary school teachers will be abolished in April. Scale 2 gives men £168 p.a.(min), £330 p.a. (max), and women £150 p.a.(min), £258 p.a.(max).

■ Golden quartzite as used in the tomb of **Tutankhamun** will be used around the swimming pool of the new liner *Queen Mary*, due to be launched later this year.

15 Wednesday

Rudyard Kipling is fighting for his life.

■ The BBC announces that it hopes to carry out test **television** transmissions from Alexandra Palace in March.

■ Nearly 200 passengers escape death in a **train crash** when the 5.22pm from Liverpool Street Station to Chingford overruns the buffers at Chingford. Two people are slightly injured.

... 1935 was the best year for TRADE since the world slump. Export sales were £33,957,851 over the previous year, according to figures out today ...

16 Thursday

Britain does not commit herself to the **oil embargo** on Italy.

■ Messrs Shippam of Chichester, famous for their potted meats, etc. have offered to pay an extra 2s. per ton for coal, provided the money goes to increase miners' wages and there will be no strike.

■ The Cornish night express runs into part of a coal train at Shrivenham, Wilts. The driver and a woman passenger are killed and many others are injured.

■ 90,000 people so far have visited the

FUN SPOT

Useless Eustace

"They're moth-balls, Winnie. I thought I'd better do something. I've had an awful lot of holes in my socks just lately!"

exhibition of the Duke and Duchess of Gloucester's **wedding presents** at St James's Palace, and have bought 15,000 catalogues, the profits from which will go to charity.

17 Friday

Twenty million mourning stamps for **Queen Astrid** of Belgium are expected to be sold by the Belgian authorities before the issue is withdrawn.
■ Italian war-planes bomb Red Cross units in Abyssinia.
. . . Professor Albert Einstein applies for American citizenship . . .
■ France warns Germany to keep out of the demilitarized zone of the Rhineland.
■ Bruno Hauptmann is granted a 30-day stay of execution.

18 Saturday

Rudyard Kipling (70), *left,* dies. Probably the most famous and successful British writer of his time and the unofficial poet laureate, he refused all honours, even the OM. UK sales of his books are estimated at four million copies. The British Museum reveals that in 1925 Rudyard Kipling presented it with the autograph manuscript of *Kim*, and another of poems, but the gift was not to be made known until after his death.
■ The British research ship *Discovery II* radios from the Bay of Whales, Antarctica to report that **Lincoln Ellsworth**, *pictured, top*, the famous US explorer, and his pilot Herbert Hollick Kenyon have been found alive after being missing for two months. They succeeded in their objective to fly

2,440 miles across the Antarctic, but ran out of fuel 20 miles from their base and have been marooned for eight weeks.
. . . SNOW sweeps Britain.

19 Sunday

Crowds gather outside Buckingham Palace all day to read the bulletins on *the* King's health. The King appoints Counsellors of State to act for him. Shortly before midnight, the **King dies** of bronchial pneumonia. **Edward VIII** accedes to the throne.
■ The **Aga Khan** is weighed in gold to celebrate his Golden Jubilee at a Durbar in Bombay. At 16 stone, he is worth £25,125, which he gives to welfare work.

20 Monday

Edward VIII is proclaimed King. Mrs Wallis Simpson and other friends watch the proclamation from a window of St James's Palace.
■ **Rudyard Kipling** is to be buried in Poets' Corner at Westminster Abbey.
■ The oldest and most revered Coptic Church in Abyssinia proclaims the King of Italy its earthly protector and patron in place of the Emperor of **Abyssinia**. This is tantamount to excommunication of the Emperor. Holy men, hermits and elders offer up thanks for Italy's intervention in Abyssinia.
. . . Philosopher BERTRAND RUSSELL marries his third wife, his former secretary Patricia Spence . . .

21 Tuesday

The royal princes fly back to Norfolk. The body of King George V is pulled on a **hand bier** from the house to Sandringham Church, (picture, page 8) followed by Queen

Mary with the Duke of Kent and the Earl of Harewood. The Princess Royal and the Duchess of Kent follow behind. The late King's piper plays the *Flowers of the Forest*. The procession makes its solemn way to the church at **Sandringham**, *above*.

22 Wednesday

The public are asked to go into mourning —a black armband or tie is sufficient—until next Tuesday's funeral.

■ In France, the Laval government resigns.

■ Copies of *The Times* newspaper are confiscated in Frankfurt, because of the Munich correspondent's article on Catholic and Jewish problems in Munich.

■ The Bodleian Library in Oxford reveals that Rudyard Kipling gave it the autograph manuscript of *Puck of Pook's Hill*, on condition that it was not shown before his death.

. . . Intense cold in the mid-West states of the USA. 47°F below zero in Thief River Falls, Minnesota.

23 Thursday

The body of King George V is taken from Sandringham by train to Westminster where he will **lie in state**. His four sons stand through the early hours of the morning between the officers of the household brigade.

. . . SNOW sweeps across the British Isles. Battered by 100mph winds, the Nantucket Lightship off Massachusetts, USA, is torn from her moorings. Eleven men are aboard.

24 Friday
New Moon

The King decrees that the day of the funeral will not be a day of public mourning.

■ Famous contralto, **Dame Clara Butt** (62), *right*, dies at her home in Oxfordshire.

■ **Blizzards** sweep across eastern Canada. Roads are blocked with snowdrifts six feet high. 74° of frost recorded at White River, Ontario. In New York the cold weather continues and 75 deaths have been recorded so far. It is so cold the street sweepers refuse to work.

■ M Albert Sarraut is the new French premier.

25 Saturday

The **miners' strike** is off as miners reluctantly accept the owners' offer. S.Wales miners get an increased minimum percentage on basic rates from 22½ per cent to 25 per cent, with subsistence of 7s. 8d. a day to be increased by 5d.

■ European Figure Skating championships end watched by General Goering. **Sonja Henie** of Norway successfully defends her women's title for a ninth time. Cecilia Colledge (15) of England is second. Karl Schaefer of Austria is the top man.

26 Sunday

Foundation Day, Australia.

Heatwave in South Africa. It's 112°F in the shade.
■ The 110,000 members of the Reich Association of German Anglers will wear uniform from now on. It is a grey-green suit with a dark green collar and a badge bearing the association's crest in silver. Officers will have badges of rank. The chief stamp-collecting clubs were recently organized into a Reich organization of Philatelists, but so far, it is believed, without a uniform.

27 Monday

A K Quist (Aus) wins the Australian singles' title, beating the holder J H Crawford 6-2, 6-3, 4-6, 3-6, 9-7. It is the third title Quist has won from Crawford this year.
■ A huge **steel bell** weighing ten and a half tons and 7ft 6ins high is presented to Dr Lewald, president of the Olympiad Organizing Committee in Berlin by the bell foundry at Bochum. It will be heard for the first time when Herr Hitler opens the Olympic Games.

28 Tuesday

King's funeral: 500 people faint, or are injured, in the crush at Marble Arch both before the procession arrives and as the King is passing. Nearly a million people file past the coffin during the lying-in-state.
■ **Adolf Hitler** attends a service at noon in memory of George V at the English church of St George in Berlin.
■ Employment exchanges are open until 11 o'clock then close for the rest of the day.

29 Wednesday

Floods in the home counties, Notts, Leics, Essex and the West country.
■ Mussolini lays the foundation stone of the cinema city to be built

three and a half miles outside the Porta San Giovanni, Rome. 45 different buildings will be spread over 600,000 square metres.
■ A memorial to Col T E **Lawrence of Arabia**, *right,* is unveiled in St Paul's Cathedral by Lord Halifax.
. . . A first edition of *Vanity Fair* **in its original 20 parts is sold in New York for $3,500 [£700] . . .**
■ Germany pledges no violation of the Rhineland.

30 Thursday

There are queues outside Windsor Castle to see the wreaths laid on the lawns outside St George's Chapel.
■ Gangs of workmen are busy in Hyde Park clearing the the 31 tons of rubbish left behind by the crowd watching the funeral of King George V.
■ **Jack Petersen**, the holder, beats **Len Harvey** on points to retain the British and Empire Heavyweight title at Wembley.

31 Friday

Heavy rain and **flooding** in many parts of England. The Thames, *below,* at Temple, is a threatening 2ft 5ins above its normal high-tide levels.
■ By Order of Council, the Prayer Book is to be amended to include prayers for King Edward, Queen Mary and the Duke and Duchess of York.
. . . The SCHOOL LEAVING AGE is to be raised to 15 on September 1, 1939 . . .
■ The advance party of the 2nd Mount Everest expedition led by **Hugh Ruttledge** leaves England for Darjeeling.

A Family – and a Nation – in Mourning as the King is Laid to Rest

REPORTS that King George V is suffering from pneumonia and is confined to bed appear on January 17. Next day, it is confirmed that he is seriously ill. He dies shortly before midnight on the 19th.

King Edward VIII orders 9 months' court mourning and flags fly at half-mast in Paris. France orders 30 days' mourning, Italy 2 weeks, Denmark 3 weeks, and the NY Stock Exchange closes as a mark of respect. Messages of sympathy pour in from around the world, and tom-toms spread the news throughout Africa. The King lies in state in Westminster Hall for five days. On Tuesday 28th, 124 naval ratings pull the gun carriage bearing the King's body through the streets from Westminster to Paddington Station for the funeral service at St George's Chapel, Windsor.

Kings, princes and politicians from 47 countries attend the service, and King Edward VIII sprinkles a handful of earth on his father's coffin as it is lowered into the vault. The service is broadcast all around the world.

GEORGE V 1865-1936
Reigned from 1910

FEBRUARY

1 Saturday

There are 2,581,027 registered cars on the road—an increase of 17.5% on 1934.

■ From today passengers on long-distance trains will be able to send telegrams to anywhere in the UK and Ireland.

■ **Lord Derby** is leasing the royal race-horses until the end of the racing year, but the King has every intention of continuing his racing stables and the royal stud when the period of mourning is over.

... Scotland v Wales RUGBY match at Murrayfield ends in victory for Wales, 13-3 ...

2 Sunday

10,000 new de luxe **pens with steel nibs** have been issued by the Post Office. The nib can only be removed with pliers, to prevent the losses that occurred when the pens were first supplied in 1929. So great is the appreciation of the new pens that their active life varies from two weeks in Edinburgh to six months in Chippenham and Frome, and an estimated five years in Newcastle-upon-Tyne, where the pens are chained.

■ There are no flights out of Croydon for the continent because of snow and ice.

■ **Queen Mary**, *left*, and the **Princess Royal,** dressed in black and accompanied by the Earl of Harewood and King Haakon of Norway, leave Buckingham Palace for the first time since the King's funeral and drive to lunch with the Duke and Duchess of Gloucester.

■ **Strike** at Smithfield Meat Market.

3 Monday

The new Geological Museum in Kensington, which opened last July, has had 159,000 visitors in six months, against 18-20,000 per year in the old premises in Jermyn Street.

To the Daily Mirror love Shirley Temple

FILMS OF THE YEAR

Rembrandt	Charles Laughton, Elsa Lanchester, Gertrude Lawrence
Modern Times	Charlie Chaplin, Paulette Goddard
A Tale Of Two Cities	Ronald Colman
Mr Deeds Goes to Town	Gary Cooper
Mutiny on the Bounty	Charles Laughton, Clark Gable
A Night at the Opera	The Marx Brothers
Charge of the Light Brigade	Errol Flynn, Patric Knowles, Olivia de Havilland
Libelled Lady	William Powell, Spencer Tracey, Myrna Loy, Jean Harlow
Our Relations	Laurel and Hardy
The Garden of Allah	Joel Macrae, Marlene Dietrich
Last of the Mohicans	Randolph Scott, Binnie Barnes
Thank You, Jeeves	David Niven, Arthur Treacher
Go West Young Man	Mae West
Story of Louis Pasteur	Paul Muni
Dimples	Shirley Temple
Windbag the Sailor	Will Hay, Graham Moffat, Moore Marriott
The Jungle Princess	Dorothy Lamour

Top left: Gertrude Lawrence and Charles Laughton as they appear in *Rembrandt.* **Bottom left:** *Dimples* **herself, otherwise known as Shirley Temple. Top right: Clark Gable. Above: Marlene Dietrich and Ronald Colman. Right: Scenes from** *A Night at the Opera* **and** *A Tale of Two Cities*.

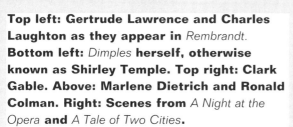

■ London is without **meat** because of the strike at Smithfield.

■ Snowstorms sweep south. No break in the freezing weather in America. Tangiers Island in Chesapeake Bay has been unreachable by sea for 14 days.

. . . UNEMPLOYMENT figures for January show a total of 2,159,722 — down 165,651 on last year . . .

■ Four and a half million people in Britain spend only 4s. each a week on food according to Sir John Boyd Orr, a member of the **Diet of the People Committee**, which means that their diet is deficient for health and can cause stunted growth in children.

4 Tuesday

Workmen are trying to stop Richmond Hill, Surrey, from slipping. Thousands of tons of earth are moving slowly towards the river, tearing up ornamental stonework and trees.

■ **Max Factor**, *below*, the make-up king of Hollywood, who learnt his trade with the Imperial Ballet in Russia, is opening in London. His laboratory will be at Park Royal, and he'll have a studio in Old Bond Street.

. . . London MEAT STRIKE continues. Remaining supplies will be sold out in a day or two.

5 Wednesday

Niagara Falls is **solid ice** for the first time in living memory.

■ There are riots at the opening of **Charlie Chaplin's** latest film *Modern Times* in New York. Traffic in Times Square is brought to a halt for 15 mins. It is the first Chaplin film for five years, and has taken two years to film at a cost of £400,000. *(See panel, facing).*

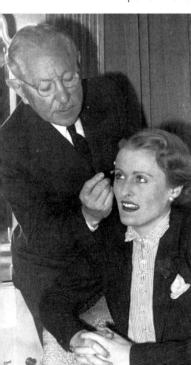

6 Thursday

Ft Lt Tommy Rose, *above,* leaves Lympne Airport on the first leg of his flight to Capetown. He hopes to set a new record . . .

■ Adolf Hitler opens the 4th **Winter Olympics** at Garmisch Partenkirchen. Each team dips its national flag before Herr Hitler, who acknowledges with the Nazi salute

■ On St Valentine's Day, every employee of the Chrysler Motor Company will receive a valentine from Walter P Chrysler of a week's salary and a bonus for every year of service to mark the close of the best year in the firm's history. The total will exceed £400,000 for the 60,000 employees worldwide.

7 Friday
Full Moon

Jarwahalal Nehru is elected president of the Indian National Congress which effectively makes him Gandhi's heir-apparent.

■ Boxer dogs—a German breed between a bulldog and a hound—will be shown in Britain for the first time at **Cruft's Dog Show** next week.

THOROUGHLY MODERN CHARLIE

Charlie Chaplin has a great success with his satire on industrialisation, Modern Times, though, as a silent film, it runs against the trends. Critics see in it the 'sinister arm of Communism', and it is banned in Germany and Italy. Paulette Goddard, soon to be Mrs Chaplin, also stars in the movie.

■ **Sir Oswald Mosley** is awarded ½d. damages and no costs in his suit against the General Secretary of the NUR who, he alleges, slandered him in a speech.

■ **Greta Garbo**, skiing in Sweden, intends to return to Hollywood to oversee the filming of *The Lady of the Camellias*, says her brother. There is no truth in the rumours that she has had a nervous breakdown, is suffering from religious mania or has financial worries.

. . . Washington is buried under 16ins of snow . . .

8 Saturday

The Scottish Nationalist Party petitions the King. They want him to refrain from using the wrong title and to use Edward VIII of England and II of Scotland.

■ The German Foreign Minister apologises to the British Ambassador for the arrest of an English woman (a director of Universal Aunts) on a visit to Germany who was taken into custody when she refused to give the Nazi salute at a meeting in Munich. He also apologises to the lady involved.

■ A P Herbert, the independent MP for Oxford University, has three Bills before the House of Commons including one on reform of the divorce law.

9 Sunday

The **War Debt** still owed by France to the UK is £755,875,000.

■ **Fl Lt Tommy Rose** arrives in Capetown from Lympne setting a **new record** of 3days 17hrs and 38mins.

■ A fire at **Elstree Film Studios** causes £450,000 worth of damage. Cameraman Ronnie Neame films the blaze while hundreds of people watch, among them Anna Neagle, Clive Brook and Herbert Wilcox. All the films were saved, and work will resume immediately.

. . . The MEAT STRIKE is over!

FEBRUARY

10 Monday

100mph gales lash the coast. At Shoeburyness, Essex, the sea foam is frozen solid. Ten people die in Britain's coldest weather for years. Since January 1,500 people in the USA have died of cold.

11 Tuesday

Dame Laura Knight becomes the first woman to be appointed an RA.

■ The BBC announces that the biggest theatre organ in the world will be installed in St George's Hall, London.

■ The opening in London of **Charlie Chaplin**'s film, *Modern Times*. It is so popular that stars such as Charles Laughton and Maurice Chevalier cannot get in.

12 Wednesday

The **St Neots Quads,** (Ernest, Anne, Michael and Paul), *left,* the first quads in 100 years to survive, are going to be film stars. Gaumont British has given them a five-year contract to make regular screen appearances.

■ Film stars **Jackie Coogan** (20) and his fiancée **Betty Grable** (19) are held up and robbed by a masked gunman in their Chicago hotel. Under her contract Miss Grable cannot marry until she is 21, but then she and Jackie, to use his own words, are going to 'go to it'.

13 Thursday

Mouths of **rivers** and creeks along the coast are **frozen** over and shipping is unable to move. A barge has been fitted as an ice breaker on the Grand Union Canal at Tring.

■ Professor Julian Huxley, at a lunch at the National Institute of Industrial Psychology, says that Britain needs a **diet** dictator. The average person needs to increase consumption of eggs, fruit, vegetables and meat, and would gain 2ins in height and 6-8lbs in weight.

■ **Leon Blum**, *left*, the French socialist leader, is attacked in Paris by members of a royalist organization, but escapes without serious injury.

... **A red Chow wins the Best in Show at the Crufts Dog Show.** ...

■ Second reading of the Education Bill which proposes raising the school leaving age to 15.

14 Friday

When the Cunard White Star liner **Queen Mary** is launched, she will fly a flag at her stern made by more than 300 girls attached to the Queen Mary School at Lytham St Anne's. The Head thought Lancashire should have a hand in the ship, wrote to Cunard, and they accepted her offer.

■ Mr Arthur Neve of Mildenhall, Suffolk, has 51 jobs—an accountant, journalist, income tax collector, newspaper manager, clerk to the council, etc. His jobs include dozens of chairmanships and secretaryships; he reckons he works 3 days a week for the public.

15 Saturday

The New York Philharmonic report that Arturo Toscanini has resigned as conductor. He will conduct the orchestra for the last time on April 26.

... **A PIGEON lost by Mr Palmer of Chudleigh, Devon, in 1929 has just returned home** ...

■ **Prosperity** is returning to Clydebank. Apart from the *Queen Mary*, 92 vessels are on order or under construction.

16 Sunday

The Union Castle liner *Winchester Castle*, bound for Port Natal with 388 passengers on board runs aground at Portland, Dorset, in thick fog. Three destroyers and the Weymouth lifeboat are called out.

■ The roof of Merton College, Oxford, one of the oldest colleges, catches fire. Dons and **undergraduates fight the flames**, fanned by the wind, which travel along the

1936 FACT FILE

UK population	544,500,000 (468 per sq mile)
UK area (including Irish Free State)	121,463 sq miles
British Empire Area	13,900,782 sq miles
British Empire polulation	493,370,000
Head of State	King George V (until Jan. 19)
(Year of the three Kings)	King Edward VIII (until Dec 10)
	King George VI
Prime Minister	**Stanley Baldwin** (Con), *right*
UK Marriages	580,042
UK Births	720,129
UK Deaths	400,619
Archbishop of Canterbury	Cosmo Gordon Lang
Astronomer Royal	H Spencer Jones
Astronomer Royal (Scotland)	R A Sampson
Number of telephones	2,826 995
Number of houses built	339,538
Licensed Motor Vehicles	2,581,027

wooden beams under the tiles. The building is saved.

■ Great Britain ends Canadian domination of Ice Hockey at the Winter Olympics by winning the **gold medal**. It's the first time the Canadians have been beaten since 1920. Most of the British team are Canadians of British parentage!

17 Monday

The **British Industries Fair** opens in London and Birmingham. It is the largest ever staged in this country with over 23 miles of stands and 3,000 exhibitors. Buyers from 64 foreign countries and overseas dominions

are attending. Novelties include an egg-grading machine that can process 3,600 eggs an hour, a cocktail tray that can be held in any position without spilling anything and flowers made from ostrich feathers.

18 Tuesday

Charlie Chaplin's film *Modern Times* is banned in Germany. A Nazi spokesman says it has communist tendencies, but it is thought that similarities in the moustache might be the real reason for the film's ban.

■ The **finger-print laboratory** at Scotland Yard has a million prints in its Criminal Record Office, and although dead men's prints are destroyed every week, it is overflowing. This criminal Who's Who is regarded as the finest register of its kind in the world.

19 Wednesday

Olympic champion **Sonja Henie,** *left,* says she will never become a professional. On a

BOOKS OF THE YEAR

Oil Paint And Grease Paint	Laura Knight
George V	Arthur Bryant
Dramatis Personae	W B Yeats
Anatomy of Frustration	H G Wells
In Praise of Idleness	Bertrand Russell
The Torch of Freedom	Stanley Baldwin
Essays Ancient And Modern	T S Eliot
Abinger Harvest	E M Forster
As I Was Saying	G K Chesterton
Sagittarius Rising	C Day Lewis
South Riding	Winifred Holtby
Jamaica Inn	Daphne du Maurier
The World Over	Edith Wharton
Eyeless in Gaza	Aldous Huxley
Island Of Sheep	John Buchan
Novel On Yellow Paper	Stevie Smith
The Weather In The Streets	Rosamund Lehmann
Murder in Mesopotamia	Agatha Christie
Flowers For The Judge	Margery Allingham
Green Hills of Africa	Ernest Hemingway
News From Tartary	Peter Fleming

Top Authors: (clockwise from top left) Laura Knight, Ernest Hemingway, Daphne Du Maurier and G K Chesterton.

train to Paris where she will take part in the World figure-skating championships, she reveals she has been offered $100,000 for a 10-month tour of the United States.
■ German Nazi organizations are banned from Switzerland after the assassination of the Nazi **spy** chief Herr Gustoff.

20 Thursday

Secret talks in Rome fuel fears of an Italo-German alliance.
■ **Black bees** from Umgogumtshani, S Rhodesia, which don't sting and are said to produce some of the world's finest honey, have arrived at London Zoo where efforts will be made to acclimatise them.
■ London's first restaurant theatre, formerly the Prince Edward Theatre, will open in March. It will be called the London Casino and the opening show will be *Folies Parisiennes* from the Casino at Miami, Florida, USA.

21 Friday

Premier Azana of Spain orders an amnesty for 30,000 political prisoners. The Communists, furious at being excluded from the government, are already seeking to undermine it. The government is composed almost entirely of personal friends of the premier.
■ Ellen Wilkinson, socialist MP for Jarrow, causes a sensation in a House of Commons Standing Committee by **smoking** a cigarette. The chairman rules her out of order and asks her to desist.
■ **Road casualties** last week are the lowest ever recorded since the Ministry of Transport started issuing figures: 94 deaths and 2,748 injuries.

22 Saturday
New Moon

The Football League have plans to cripple the **football pools** by scrapping the remainder of fixtures for the season and

rearranging them secretly so that the pools companies cannot use the advance fixture lists. A scheme has been put forward to charge pools promoters a reproduction fee.
■ **Sonja Henie** retains her World Figure Skating championship for the tenth time, beating Megan Taylor of Great Britain. She has also been European champion ten times and Olympic champion three times. She says she will now retire.

23 Sunday

Spain celebrates the victory of the Leftists.
■ The **Thames overflows** at Twickenham. And, at 3ft 7ins above its normal level, comes close to flooding the Embankment in central London. There is 4ins snow in Leeds and 6ins in Bradford.

24 Monday

Football clubs revolt against the pools war.
■ It is thought that the possibility of an Italo-German Front is no longer likely and that the German ambassador has presented Mussolini with a blunt refusal.
■ A report published today by the Department of Science and Industrial Research says **pollution** by smoke and sulphur is growing worse.
■ Sir Thomas Beecham makes his peace with Brighton by conducting the London Philharmonic Orchestra in the new Dome, which he bitterly criticized at its opening six months ago.

25 Tuesday

Latest fashion for men — shirts made from dog hair. (Collies provide the best.)

■ Bradford is a city without light following an **explosion** in the corporation's electricity works last night. No cinemas are open and factory workers have to be sent home.
... There is an attempted Army coup d'etat in TOKYO led by Captain Teruso Ando..
■ The **King**'s racehorse *Marconi*, in Lord Derby's colours, wins the Saltley Chase in Birmingham. It is

the first win under his leasing agreement with the King.

26 Wednesday
Ash Wednesday

The **Volkswagen,** or 'People's car', *above*, designed by Ferdinand Porsche, goes into production at a factory in Saxony opened today by Adolf Hitler. It has a top speed of 50mph and will cost £70 to purchase.
■ Actress Wendy Hiller becomes an overnight sensation in New York in *Love on the Dole*.

27 Thursday

The funeral of King George V cost £250,000.
■ Adolf **Hitler's sister**, Angela Raubel, marries Dr Martin Hammisch in Berlin. Herr Hitler is not present at the wedding, and the wedding was not reported in the German press. His sister, who has been married before, was Hitler's housekeeper at Berchtesgaden.
■ Football pools promoters believe they have solved their problems with the League.
... The death is announced of DR IVAN PAVLOV (85), physiologist, noted for his work on the brain ...

28 Friday

The coup d'etat in Tokyo collapses when Captain Ando and his followers surrender.
■ A New York buyer has bought the entire supply (144,000) of an apple-shaped briar Maltese pipe that the King admired at the British Industries Fair. A special window display will be made in New York. Malta will be kept busy for 12 months, the pipe works will be extended and they will take on 25% more workers.
■ Hugh Ruttledge, the leader of the Everest Expedition, and his party arrive in Darjeeling.

29 Friday

London Zoo **Pet's Corner** is opening a small shop to sell guinea pigs, hamsters, white rats, rabbits and goldfish plus advice on food and rearing. The Zoo is also to have its own post office.
■ First demonstration in **Selfridges** of the first **television phone**, the Visaphone. A man on the 4th floor can be seen on a small screen on the floor below.
■ President Roosevelt signs the second Nationality Bill, which bans financial loans to countries at war.

MARCH

1 Sunday
St David's Day

Miss Dorothy Paget's **Golden Miller**, *right*, wins the Cheltenham Gold Cup by 12 lengths. It is the horse's fifth successive victory in National Hunt's premier race.
■ Edward VIII makes his **first broadcast as King** to the Empire and 11 foreign countries — Sweden, Denmark, Norway, France, USA, Poland, Austria, Hungary, Switzerland, Argentina and Brazil at 4pm

GMT. In London, concerts at the Queen's Hall and the London Palladium are interrupted to allow the message to be heard by the audiences there.

2 Monday

The League of Nations announces enforcement of an **oil embargo** on Italy.
■ The **electrification** is announced of Southern Railway from London to Portsmouth at a cost of £3,000,000. It will be completed by July 1937.
■ The Oxford **Boat Race** crew is training on beer. It has been rumoured that they were switching to champagne this year in the hope of beating Cambridge's unbroken run of success since 1923.

GERMANS ENTER RHINELAND

MAR 8 Around 10,000 Goose-stepping Germans, led by a monocled officer carrying a bunch of flowers, march into the Rhineland, ignoring the treaties of Versailles and Locarno.

France demands that Germany withdraws, but the British government urges France to do nothing until Hitler's actions 'have been given full consideration'.
Paris calls an emergency meeting of the signatories of the Locarno Treaty.

3 Tuesday

A new section of **Western Avenue**, the arterial road from Shepherd's Bush to Denham, Bucks opens. It is now possible to drive from Wood Lane, Shepherds Bush to within two miles of Uxbridge, clear of the tramlines and congestion of Ealing.
... Mussolini nationalizes the Italian banks...
■ **PanAm** will make 20 trial Transatlantic flights this year: 10 from New York to Copenhagen and 10 the other way with connections to the UK and Norway. The mail service will be in operation by mid-1937.
■ State of **Emergency** declared in **New York** by Mayor La Guardia following a strike by lift operators, furnacemen and hotel maids. Thousands of people in upper-storey apartments are deprived of medical aid, heat and hot water. The Mayor has ordered municipal employees including the police and firemen to man the lifts of all dwellings more than six storeys high.

4 Wednesday

Radium is cheaper because of the discovery of ore at Great Bear Lake, Canada. Until now the Belgian Congo has had a virtual monopoly. The price has come down from £14,000 to £8,000 per gramme.
■ Elsie Boobyer, a local farmer's daughter, pays £1,350 for the right to levy **tolls** for 12 months on all vehicles crossing the River Parrett at Burrowbridge, Somerset.
■ A Government White Paper reveals massive expansion in Britain's **defences** including two new capital ships, 20 new cruisers, 2,110 first line planes, four new infantry battalions, and the organization of industry for a rapid changeover to war production.

5 Thursday

The Smithfield men accept an offer of a 45-hour week, paid bank and statutory holidays, one week's paid holiday, £4 minimum wage for regular workers £3.10s. for humpers.
■ The **Spitfire Mark I** goes on show at Eastleigh Aerodrome, Southampton.
. . . The King inspects the liner Queen Mary on Clydeside . . .
■ The **Zeppelin** LZ 129 (the *Hindenburg*), *above*, takes off from Friedrichshafen with 85 people on board for a 3hr 3min flight around Lake Constanz. It will fly for eight hours tomorrow to get its certificate of airworthiness.
■ The British Everest party leaves on its 300 mile march across Tibet to the base camp on the Rongbuk Glacier.

6 Friday

80,000 liftmen, furnacemen and hotel maids are now on strike in New York, and 6,000 buildings are affected. Actress **Beatrice Lillie** is manning the switchboard at her block of flats, and playwright Charles McArthur, husband of actress Helen Hayes, is working as a furnaceman.
■ Football **pools chaos** reigns (see February 22) as only two fixtures for tomorrow are known.

. . . The second ROYAL STURGEON caught within a week, a 6ft specimen weighing 56lbs, is landed at Newlyn and accepted by the King . . .

7 Saturday

The stars are out in Hollywood for the Oscars ceremony *(see panel below)*.
■ The ambassadors of Britain, France, Italy and Belgium, signatories of the Locarno Pact, are summoned to the Reichstag expecting to hear that Germany intends to repudiate the Locarno Pact and reoccupy the Rhineland.

8 Sunday
Full Moon

German troops march into the Rhineland

WHO'S TOPS AT THE OSCARS . . .

The Informer **scoops the top Academy Awards. It gets Best Actor, Victor McLaglan, and Best Director, John Ford. Best Actress goes to Bette Davis, for Dangerous. The Best Film is** *Mutiny on the Bounty.*

(see panel, page 21). **Hitler** has proposed a new treaty to guarantee peace for 25 years, which the British regard as evidence of his good intentions.

■ The main body of porters for the Everest expedition leave for Kalimpong. Two of the porters travel by motor car, having negotiated good pay rates, and cause a sensation.

■ 200,000 people arrive by bus, ferry, car and train to see the *Queen Mary*, from any viewpoint they can find in Renfrew and Inchinnan.

9 Monday

A reduction in the cost of long-distance **phone calls** means that there is a maximum charge of 2s.6d. for 3mins in England, Wales and Scotland between 5am and 7pm, and charges are reduced in the morning between 5am and 2pm.

■ The engagement is announced in Shanghai between **Charlie Chaplin** (46) and **Paulette Goddard** (25), *right*, former chorus girl and his co-star in *Modern Times*. She will be his third wife.

. . . Ft Lt TOMMY ROSE lands at Croydon from Capetown in record-breaking time. His flight time of 6 days 6hr 57min beats the old record by 5hr 6min.

10 Tuesday

Giant profiles of presidents Washington and Jefferson have been sculpted out of rock on **Mount Rushmore**, South Dakota, USA.

■ Britain warns Germany that she will act against any act of aggression against France and Belgium which would constitute a violation of the Locarno Pact. There are now 40,000 German troops in the Rhineland.

■ The Football League's dispute with the pools firms that has caused two weeks of chaos, is over. Normal fixtures on Saturday.

11 Wednesday

The Council of the League of Nations will meet in London on Saturday to discuss Germany's re-arming of the Rhineland.

■ The second of two new single-seater monoplanes from Vickers designed for the RAF, has made its first flight. Although

details are secret, the new planes are known to be superior to anything else presently in the air.

. . . UNSEASONABLY WARM: It's 62°F at Tunbridge Wells.

12 Thursday

The Victualling Supervisor of the Cunard Fleet estimates that in one year the *Queen Mary* will require 1 million lbs beef; 40,000lbs fish; 42,000 galls milk; 6,400 galls cream; 165,000lbs butter; 22,000 galls draught lager; 21,000 bottles whisky; 725,000 bottles beer; 285,000 bottles mineral water; 11,600 bottles liqueurs; 2,000 bottles brandy; 5,800 bottles gin and 20,000 bottles champagne for its average daily population of 3,000. Nearly 400 different foodstuffs will be stored on board.

■ Twelve new **aeroplanes** complete with sleeping berths for 20 people are being built by Armstrong Whitworth for Imperial Airways. Together with the 29 flying boats already on the fleet, Imperial will have 41 passenger planes.

. . . The Ministry of Transport approves a BY-PASS

scheme for Crawley, Sussex at an estimated cost of £133,000.

■ Earthquake in Scotland at Comrie, Central Perthshire. Hundreds of shocks have been recorded here and it is the centre of British earthquakes.

13 Friday

Sir Thomas Inskip is appointed Minister of Coordination for Defence — a new appointment.

■ The *Queen Mary* will leave Clydebank on the 24th, sail down the Clyde into the North Channel and the Irish Sea, down to the Lizard, around to Spithead and reach Southampton on March 27, when tugs will take two hours to dock her. She will stay for five days. Special trains will run from London to Southampton all the time she is there. Millions of visitors are expected.

. . . JOCK MCELVOY, the British Middleweight champion, is beaten on points by John Henry Lewis (USA) in the World Cruiserweight Championship in New York.

14 Saturday

Hiking is becoming a popular leisure activity, says the Youth Hostels Association. It now has a membership of over 48,000, and 239 hostels in the UK. Another hostel will open in England this year. There are international hostels in Holland, Germany and the USA.

■ Fierce **fighting in Madrid,** *above,* as the police and communists open fire on each other. Five big churches and the offices of the Monarchist newspaper *La Nacion* are set ablaze.

■ The first round-Germany flight by the Zeppelin LZ 129 (the *Hindenburg*) is postponed.

15 Sunday

The average lifespan in the UK has increased by seven years since 1911.

TERROR ON THE STREETS OF MADRID

■ In a speech last night, **Winston Churchill** said that France's offer to submit the Franco-Soviet Pact (which Hitler felt justified Germany reoccupying the Rhineland) to the World Court at the Hague should be accepted. Churchill warns that, 'if the League of Nations is destroyed . . . and the triumph of the Nazi regime proclaimed throughout the world, events will continue to roll and slide remorselessly downhill towards the pit in which Western civilisation may be fatally engulfed.'

■ Dr Wilhelm Furtwangler whose appointment to succeed **Toscanini** as conductor of the New York Philharmonic Orchestra was announced two weeks ago, is not going to take up the position. Various groups, including several Jewish organizations, objected to his selection.

16 Monday

New York liftmen, furnacemen and hotel maids are returning to work (see March 6).

■ 37 tons of **cement** have been carried back and forth between Douglas, Isle of Man and Liverpool for more than a week because two workmen at the company in Douglas to which the cement is consigned refuse to join the TGWU, and dockers refuse to handle the cement.

■ The British Oxygen Company selects a site near Fort William for the first calcium carbide factory to be established in Scotland, as it hopes its position will reduce the risk of air attack.

17 Tuesday
St Patrick's Day

The VC of the Lifeboat service, a gold medal, is awarded to Coxswain Patrick Sliney of the Ballycotton, Co Cork lifeboat. Silver medals go to the second coxswain and motor mechanic, and bronze medals to each of the other four members of the crew, and a cash award of £19.8s.6d. for **outstanding bravery** in rescuing the crew of the Daunt's Rock Lightship, which broke loose on February 11 in heavy seas with eight men on board. From the time the lifeboat was called out until it finally returned to port, the crew had been on duty, without sleep for 63hr.
■ Work will begin in the next few days on the building of a cathedral at Guildford, Surrey. £42,000 has been collected so far— enough to make a start.
. . . A decree in Spain prohibits any Spaniard leaving the country with more than £140 in paper MONEY in his possession . . .

18 Wednesday

The King gives the first levee of his reign at Buckingham Palace.
■ **Sonja Henie** is reported to have turned professional. She is understood to have signed a £7,000 contract with the Madison Square Gardens Corp. to make a series of public appearances in New York, Chicago and Detroit. A film contract is also under discussion.
■ Fire brigades from 10 towns are called to a fire at **Denham Film Studios**. At one time the whole £750,000 complex was threatened. A 200yd human bucket chain carries water from the River Colne. It is the fourth fire at film premises in London in the past five months. Reconstruction work is beginning immediately.

19 Thursday

Young English actor Patric Knowles leaves for Hollywood where he will feature in the film *The Charge of the Light Brigade*, starring Errol Flynn.
■ The text is published of a Bill to set up a national service of salaried **midwives**.
■ Two new examples of the **Austin Seven** are shown off by **Sir Herbert Austin**, *left*, in Birmingham. The new model will appear at Brooklands at Easter.

20 Friday

Floods devastate 12 states in the USA. 106 are reported dead, and 200,000

homeless. The Potomac River in Washington bursts its banks.

■ Britain and France approve a programme for a new **European Peace Plan**. The League of Nations will be asked to call a world conference to discuss monetary and economic problems, and Germany will be asked to submit her complaint against the Franco-Soviet pact to the High Court. If Germany agrees, France and Belgium will withdraw their demand that German troops leave the Rhineland.

■ New buildings for Whitehall. The Ministry of Transport is the first one to be pulled down and rebuilt at an estimated cost of £1,750,000, and should be completed sometime in 1940-41. The whole lot will be finished by 1945-46. The architect is Vincent Harris, who also designed Manchester City Library, and the Bristol Council House.

PRICE LIST	
Dog licences	7s.6d. p.a.
Male servants	15s. p.a.
Car licence	£4.10s.
Driver's licence	5s.
Income tax (stand. rate)	4s.6d in £
Postage (UK)	1½d (1oz)
Imperial Air Service	1½d (½oz)
(South Africa, Kenya, Rhodesias, Uganda, Nyasaland, Tanganyika, Sudan, Zanzibar and Mauritius)	
Elsewhere	2½d (½oz)
Postcards (inland)	1d

21 Saturday

The Post Office has finished work on the Talking Clock and it will go into service on July 1. Miss Jane Cain (the voice) spent six weeks recording it.

■ **Bognor Regis** is to get a new sea front, including tennis courts, a new bandstand, improvements to the pavilion, and a children's area.

■ Martial law in many American states and grave danger of typhoid following the floods. The death toll is now 200 and homeless 250,000. Flood damage is estimated to be £40 million.

... Calcutta Cup Rugby: England beat the old enemy, Scotland 9-8 ...

■ 65°F in London, the warmest March day for FIVE years.

22 Sunday

The roof collapses at Bardykes Colliery between Blantyre and Cumbuslang,

Lanarkshire. Five men are killed.

■ Guardsman Arthur Leslie Bursell (2), of Hull, is **court-martialled** and discharged from the Army because he won't shave off his moustache.

■ **Carnival** atmosphere on the banks of the Clyde, and 10,000 stand in queues to be shown over the *Queen Mary* before she leaves for Southampton.

23 Monday
New Moon

The House of Commons proposes an increase in salaries. The Prime Minister, Stanley Baldwin, should get an increase from £5,000 to £8,000, and Cabinet Ministers should get £5,000.

■ **Megan Taylor**, British figure skating champion in 1932, 1933 and 1934, withdraws from the British Women's Figure Skating Championships in a dispute over one of the judges

... **MUSSOLINI, left, says that he will nationalize all Italy's key industries** ...

24 Tuesday
Mohammedan New Year (1355)

The liner *Queen Mary* leaves the Clyde and sails to Greenock. Tens of thousands gather on the banks and sing *Auld Lang Syne*. She runs aground twice, but sustains no damage.

■ **Measles** outbreak. In the London County Council area alone there are 100 new cases a day. 2,278 are hospitalized. 20 soldiers at Bordon Camp, Hants are suffering, too.

■ **Gordon Richards**, *right*, last year's champion jockey with 210 wins, celebrates the

WHAT'S ON AT THE THEATRE

Follow The Sun	The Cochrane Review, with Vic Oliver and Claire Luce (above, right)
Out Of The Dark	Felix Aylmer and Gwen Ffrangcon-Davies
Glamourous Nights	by Ivor Novello, with Barry Sinclair, Olive Gilbert
The Lady of La Paz	Nigel Patrick, Nova Pilbeam
St Helena	by R C Sheriff and Jeanne de Casalis, with Leo Genn and Lydia Sherwood.
The Visitor	by Nicholas Montsarrat, with Guy Middleton, Greer Garson
Careless Rapture	by Ivor Novello, with Dorothy Dickson (above, centre) Zena Dare
Murder in The Cathedral	by T S Eliot
The Amazing Dr Clitterhouse	Barry Lyndon, Ralph Richardson, Meriel Forbes
The Happy Hypocrite	by Clemence Dane, with Ivor Novello, Vivien Leigh (above left)

opening of the Flat season with a win on *Even So* in the Hainton Plate.

. . . Start of the 5th RAC RALLY from nine different points between London and Glasgow. 317 cars leave at two-minute intervals on their 1,000 mile journey to Torquay. 12 cars are entered and driven by women. . .

25 Wednesday

Hitler rejects the Anglo-French peace plan.

■ A first edition (1814) of the translation of *Swiss Family Robinson*, from the German-Swiss, is sold at Sotheby's for £225.

■ Soviet scientists claim that the eggs of a crawfish laid 1,000 years ago and buried in permafrost have been hatched out. Ten generations of normal crawfish have already been obtained.

. . . MIGRATION to Australia is to be renewed . . .

■ Opening of the *Daily Mail Ideal Home*

Exhibition by the Minister of Health, Sir Kingsley Wood. 600 firms are exhibiting.

26 Thursday

Sensational Lincolnshire Handicap won by *Over Coat* 10-1 ridden by Tommy Weston after three horses fall (one of them is destroyed).

■ The Royal Stud at Sandringham is to be closed. All the brood mares will be moved to Hampton Court.

■ The flight of the **Hindenburg** is stopped because of damage to the rudder and fin.

■ The Benedictines complete the building of Buckfast Abbey which has taken 30 years. The Lord Abbot blesses the largest bell – Hosana, weighing eight tons – before it is hoisted into the 160ft bell tower.

FASHION HIGHSPOTS OF 1936

WHAT TO WEAR . . . the eternal debate as the sporting Season gets into full swing. And the British weather only adds to a girl's dilemma. At Ascot (right) there is no option but to cover up against the elements. The hats are more functional than flamboyant. But, at Henley (below), the sun at last greets revellers, providing a chance to display cool, flowing outfits. But showers are never far away, so the raincoat is an essential accessory . . .

IF YOU want to get ahead . . . get a hat. Top left, this has something of a nautical flavour to it, with a dash of gypsy thrown in. Far right, this can only spell Ascot, which was a damp squib this year — though not quite cold enough for the persian lamb cap (centre) with matching cravat and muff.

A real contrast: a shapely cape (left), furs to keep out the cold at the Grand National (right), and (above) the latest in bathing suits, on display at Morecambe.

27 Friday

Reynoldstown, *left,* owned by Major Furlong and ridden by Fulke Walwyn, wins the Grand National for the second year running. *Golden Miller* falls at the first fence

■ A radio operator with scarlet fever has been taken off the *Queen Mary*. Members of the public can go onto the dock for a shilling, but are not allowed on board.

■ The King gives his mother, Queen Mary, the rank of Grand Master of the OBE, the first woman to hold the office.

28 Saturday

Half a ton of gold arrives from France before the bank rate in Paris is raised by one and a half per cent— indicating that France intends to continue on the **Gold Standard**.

■ A new mouth has blown out at the base of **Mt Vesuvius**, and boiling lava flows out.

29 Sunday

Germans all round the world vote **Yes** for Hitler and the Reichstag. 99% of the people respond positively to the plebiscite on Adolf Hitler — 43,353,186 for, 527,282 against.

■ The 100th anniversary of **The Pickwick Papers** is celebrated with the arrival of Mr Pickwick in Rochester by coach.

■ 16,000 people pay to visit the *Queen Mary* and 19 extra trains are put on to carry visitors from London.

30 Monday

Bruno Hauptmann's **appeal** for mercy is rejected and he is to go to the electric chair.

■ The Secretary for Mines starts the drilling at Paulsgrove, near Portsmouth, where the first attempt is to be made to produce **oil** on an industrial scale in England.

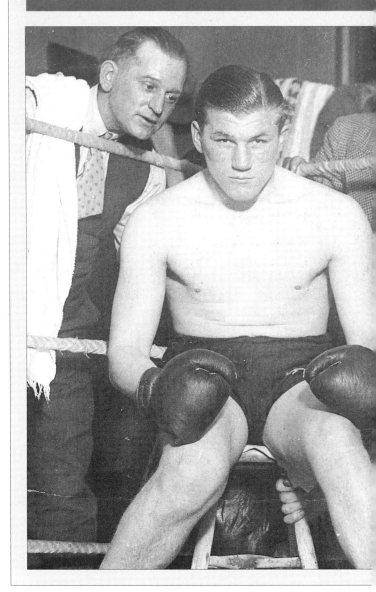

PACKING A PUNCH: THE

■ Five King penguins and four Rock Hopper penguins arrive at London Zoo from Norway, where they were cared for on a whaling ship. Keeper Flewin fed them by hand.

31 Tuesday

The **Hindenburg** leaves Friedrichshafen today on her first trip across the Atlantic to South America with 35 fare-paying passengers, a number of officials and a motor car.

LEADING RINGMASTERS OF 1936

TOMMY FARR (left), the Welsh cruiserweight champion, takes a breather during training for his fight against Tommy Loughran (USA). Len Harvey (above); Jack Petersen (right); and, (below right), Max Schmelling and Joe Louis measure up for their World heavyweight title bout.

■ The BBC will not say definitely, but the **Coronation** may be televised.
. . . The Duke of Gloucester is 36 today . . .

APRIL

1 Wednesday

Bekonscot, the model village in Beaconsfield, reopens to the public today after a face-lift with Belisha beacons and traffic lights that flash on Sundays. In its six years of operation it has raised £1,400 for the Railway Benevolent Institution.

■ 300 film actors have a narrow escape when **fire** breaks out at Lone Pine, the Warner Brothers unit film location in California. Several actors including Errol Flynn and David Niven help fight the flames.

■ The Austrian government, in violation of the treaties of Versailles and Locarno, reintroduces National Service.

2 Thursday

In the House of Commons, Ellen Wilkinson MP moves an amendment asking the government to adopt the House of Commons resolution of May 1920 to give common classes of women in the Civil Service **equal pay**.

■ **Count John McCormack** *left,* the famous Irish **tenor,** says he will retire next year, 30 years to the day he made his debut at Covent Garden in *Cavelleria Rusticana*.

■ Dr Thomes Ethelbert Page of Godalming, Surrey, famous Greek scholar and former 6th form master at Charterhouse School, the inventor of '*Oxford Bags*', dies aged 86. For half a century he wore baggy trousers of amazing cut with a black jacket and bowler hat.

... **Sonja Henie is said to have accepted £80,000 for a tour of ten US cities.**

■ Buckingham Palace announce that the Coronation will be in May next year.

■ **Tommy Farr** (22) of Tonypandy, beats Bob Olin (USA), former holder of the World Light Heavyweight Championship, on points.

3 Friday

Famous flyer **Amy Mollison** leaves Gravesend to try and beat Tommy Rose's record flight to Cape Town.

■ Britain may have to build a rival **Suez Canal**. In 1968 the Suez Canal Company's concession runs out and the request for an extension has already been refused.

■ The British Drama League is preserving on gramophone records the voices of 24 **dialect** speakers as in 20-30 yrs, they believe, we will all talk the same.

■ Bruno Hauptmann — the man who kidnapped and later killed the infant son of flying ace Charles Lindbergh — is **executed.** (Cost of death: fee for executioner £30; fee for electrical assistant £10; Expenses £1.11s; meals for executioner, his

THOSE MAGNIFICENT MEN

... **Aside from the heroics, commercial flying is taking off, with growing demands from holidaymakers and businessmen. Guess which major new airport this is ...**

Did You Guess? *It's Gatwick Airport, which opens on June 6, 1936*

(AND WOMEN) IN THEIR FLYING MACHINES . . .

In 1936, air records were shattered with monotonous regularity by an intrepid group of flyers. Top left: Jim Mollison and his French co-pilot Edouard Corniglion-Molinier. Above: Jim's wife Amy Mollison (Johnson). Top right: Beryl Markham. Right: Jean Batten.

chauffeur and assistant £2.6s. An electric chair death costs 1s.11d. in current. The trial and appeals have cost £200,000).

4 Saturday

Boat Race — **Cambridge** win again.
■ Flyer **Amy Mollison** smashes the undercarriage of her plane on landing at Colomb Bechar on the edge of the Sahara. To make a new record flight she has to reach Cape Town in two days. The present holder Tommy Rose says there is no reason why she shouldn't regain the record — she has a much faster plane than the one he flew.
■ The **Hindenburg** is now well over the Equator. Those crossing the line for the first time receive an illuminated certificate of baptism and a Zeppelin scarf pin.

5 Sunday

Abyssinia asks the British people for £1m to buy planes to fight the Italians. Later, 300 Italian planes rain death on the Abyssinians. The Emperor is said to be fleeing with 60,000 of his troops, including the Imperial Guard.
■ People who failed to vote in the German plebiscite last month lose their jobs.
■ Thousands of **morbid sightseers** throng New York streets to catch a glimpse of Bruno Hauptmann's body as it is taken on its last journey in a wicker basket to a crematorium. The undertaker drives the hearse to and fro through the streets for two hours in an attempt to shake off pursuers. The funeral service will be private.
. . . Film star Eddie Cantor has received death threats unless he stops his anti-Nazi activities . . .

6 Monday
Full Moon

750 killed and £3.5 million damage as a

tornado, the second this week, sweeps through the states of the mid south of the USA. The entire western section of the town of Tupelo, Mississippi, is razed to the ground leaving 85 dead, 1,000 injured and 4,000 homeless.
. . . Rudyard Kipling leaves £155,228 in his WILL . . .
■ The AA announces that to assist traffic flow an AA plane will cover all main exits from London this Easter.
■ Two giant **chameleons** from Madagascar have arrived at London Zoo. Their tongues are as long as their bodies, and can pick up a lizard on the far side of the cage and eat it. For the first time in years, the boat in which they travelled from Madagascar was completely clear of cockroaches by the time it reached London. The chameleons ate the last one before they arrived.

7 Tuesday

The **Nazis** have their own Germanized version of the Sermon on the Mount published by Reichsbishop Mueller, Nazi head of the Evangelical Church. In his version all words such as meek and peaceful have been replaced by more manly terms, and entirely new passages have been inserted. For example, 'Blessed are the meek; for they shall inherit the earth,' is rendered as 'Blessed is he that at all times is a good comrade; he will succeed in the world.'
■ South Africa passes the Native Representation Act, which **bans blacks** from office, but allows them to elect three whites to represent them.

8 Wednesday

There is world-wide revulsion at the report that Italian planes have spent the last four days spraying the northern frontier of **Abyssinia** with poison gas.
■ The first showing of the **talkie, A Tale of Two Cities**, *left*, starring Ronald Colman. The film employed 10,000 actors,

SELASSIE FORCED TO FLEE AS MUSSOLINI HAILS VICTORY IN ABYSSINIAN WAR

MUSSOLINI'S forces finally blast their triumphant way to Addis Ababa. The Emperor, Haile Selassie, escapes to the French port of Djibouti with his family and supporters, where they embark in a British warship and make their way to England. The King of Italy assumes the title Emperor of Abyssinia, and Mussolini acheves his dream of winning an empire. Italy begins her so-called civilizing mission, improving communications, exploiting Abyssinia's raw materials and bringing out shiploads of colonists. Far left: Loyalist defenders. Inset: Haile Selassie.

122 of them with speaking parts.
■ 18 ambassadors and all official Washington cheer for 10mins at the end of a private view of *Things to Come*. Critics say that no film has ever made such a deep impression on the USA.

9 Thursday

The start of the busiest Easter ever known, with 3,000 cars per hour leaving London.

Imperial Airways say every available plane is in service to and from Paris. 90,000 passengers use Paddington Station.
■ Stocks of **gas masks** are to be accumulated by the government and issued free of charge in areas expected to be in danger in the event of air attack.
■ The King presents **Maundy money** to 42 men and 42 women — the same number of people as his age. He is the second reigning monarch to do so in person for 250 years.

10 Friday
Good Friday

Flyer Amy Mollison arrives back from Colomb Bechar hoping to pick up spare parts, a mechanic and a co-pilot to bring her plane back.
■ For the first time ever, **debutantes** will be presented in the open air at Buckingham Palace this summer.
■ The **Hindenburg** arrives back after its successful flight to South America.

11 Saturday

An 18-year-old English boy, Peter Harvard of Sunderland, a descendant of John Harvard, founder of **Harvard** University in Massachusetts, has been invited to enrol as a student when the college celebrates its tercentenary. His parents have yet to agree.
■ The Chief Constable of Denbighshire says the only way to stop the rise in **juvenile crime** is to bring back the birch.
■ Queen Mary spends the Easter holiday at Royal Lodge, Windsor with the Duke and Duchess of York.
. . . **Actress SYLVIA SIDNEY divorces her husband of seven months, publisher Bennett Cerf, in New York. They married in October 1935, and separated in January . . .**

12 Sunday
Easter Sunday

Snow — the first at Easter for 19 years. Most of the ladies in the Easter Parade in Hyde Park are wearing furs.
■ Asked their opinions of England, and the English, 65 young people from France, Germany, Holland, Norway, India and Ireland at an International Easter Party at Buckhurst Hill Youth Hostel, Sussex, say they like English women, but don't like the badly dressed men and the cooking.

13 Monday
Easter Monday

In Derbyshire the **snow** is so thick it stops the traffic. Ice cream men switch to roasted chestnuts and roast potatoes. Penzance has 11hrs of sunshine, Lerwick 12hr.
. . . **Motor racing at Brooklands is cancelled.**
■ Seven million young Russians pledge themselves to fight for **Stalin,** should war break out.
■ Luton Town football team beats Bristol Rovers 12-0 thanks to a record **TEN goals** from forward Joe Payne.

14 Tuesday

Princess Beatrice, *left,* the youngest child of Queen Victoria, celebrates her 79th birthday today.
■ The P & O liner *Barrapool* changes course and races towards Gibraltar to take on board art **treasures** valued at £10 million from the *Ranpura* which has run ashore off Punta Mala, carrying the priceless Chinese art recently shown in London, which is not insured. The *Ranpura* was escorted as far as the Bay of Biscay by British warships, and was to pick up another at Gibraltar.

15 Wednesday

Col Lindbergh, on a visit to the British Aircraft Manufacturing Company at Hanworth, takes to the air in an Eagle three-seater cabin plane.
■ The 2,000 ton motorship *Ostmark,* built for the German airline Lufthansa, is launched at Kiel. It will serve as an ocean aerodrome for the planes flying the airmail service across the South Atlantic.
■ Film star **Merle Oberon** sues Selznick International Pictures for £25,000 because she didn't get the starring role she had been promised in the film about Florence Nightingale.

16 Thursday

A red-billed **hornbill** at London Zoo with a broken beak looked set to starve, until the toucan next door came to his rescue. She ripped a hole in the netting between them, flew down to get a piece of banana from her breakfast, and fed the hornbill. Day after day the toucan fed the hornbill until its beak was healed.

■ A 14-year-old girl finds two live 14lb **shells** in a parcel on the doorstep of her home in Plymouth and gives them to her granny as a present. The police say the shells appear to have been stolen from a government base.

17 Friday

The *Queen Mary* completes her 48-hour service trials and sweeps up the Firth of Clyde. Tomorrow she leaves for her speed trial off the Isle of Arran.

■ An off-duty detective walking in the woods at Bassett, Southampton, stumbles over a drum of **potassium cyanide** — enough to kill 10,000 people — hidden in the undergrowth. It is believed a tramp stole the bag it was in but discarded it. The poison had been taken to a house in Bassett by a vermin killer.

. . . TURKEY marches her troops into the demilitarized Dardanelles zone at dawn . . .

18 Saturday

Five London schoolboys on holiday in the Black Forest, are caught in a severe **snowstorm** and die from cold and exhaustion. Their bodies are taken to Freiburg, where eight Hitler Youths stand guard in the chapel. Of the party of 27, a further eight are in hospital, suffering from exposure and frostbite.

■ Denmark passes a law prohibiting children under seven riding bicycles alone.

19 Sunday
Summertime begins, 2 am

Eleven die and 50 are injured in renewed **rioting** between Jews and Arabs in Tel Aviv, Palestine.

■ The King meets 1,000 boy

scouts at Windsor Castle representing every county in Britain at the annual Scout Service at St George's Chapel, Windsor.

20 Monday

Adolf Hitler, the Reichschancellor, celebrates his 47th birthday and Berlin makes it a great celebration. 14,000 troops, 977 horses and 1,573 vehicles are paraded in his honour.

■ Seventeen members of the **Indian cricket team** arrive at Tilbury huddled in overcoats and with chattering teeth. They are captained by the Maharaj Kumar of Vizianagram, who was taught to play by Test stars Don Bradman and Jack Hobbs.

■ Foreign Secretary Anthony Eden threatens that Britain might quit the League of Nations if it fails to settle the war between Italy and Abyssinia.

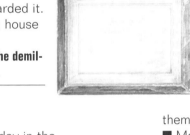

21 Tuesday
New Moon

Budget Day: An increase of 3d in the £ income tax is announced in the Chancellor's annual Budget. Tea drinkers suffer the most. It will cost them 2d. a lb more for their favourite brew.

■ Manufacturers from the south of England who have opened factories in the north say

PRINCESSES AT PLAY

Princess Elizabeth of York (right) is 10 on April 22. Among her gifts is a **new bike** from Queen Mary. Her parents have given her an electrically-propelled mini car. Left: Elizabeth – and canine friend – plays with her sister Margaret (6) in their miniature house in Windsor Great Park.

that people in the north work harder . Productivity figures are 25% higher.

■ The world's **oldest mummy** — the wife of Sechem Nefer who built the Second Pyramid 5,000 years ago — has been found by Professor Selim Hasson of Cairo.

22 Wednesday

On a farm at Walsgrave-on-Stowe, near Coventry, **milking** is done to music.
The farmer discovered that milking machines made the cows restless, but when he installed a radiogram they calmed down. The cows like waltzes best.

. . . Snow and sleet in London. At one time the temperature dropped to 38°F— 20° below normal.

23 Thursday
St George's Day

Greta Garbo leaves Stockholm to return to Hollywood to begin work on *La Dame aux Camellias* on June 15. Her new leading man will be Robert Taylor.

■ **Shirley Temple**, *left,* celebrates her seventh birthday with a circus party. She signs a new contract with Twentieth Century Fox worth £1,000 a week.

■ After 10 days in total darkness, while **rescuers** drilled through rock to find them, two men walk out of a gold mine in Moose River, Nova Scotia.

. . . JACK PETERSEN beats Jock McElvoy on points at Earls Court to retain the British and Empire Heavyweight titles. . .

24 Friday

Uproar over alleged Budget leaks.

■ Amelia Earhart, the first woman to cross the Atlantic solo, is contemplating a **round-the-world flight** from East to West. She will fly in an all-metal plane, the Lockheed Electra. She intends to make several non-stop dashes across the USA as test flights.
■ **Hermann Goering** is appointed Special Commissioner for the Reichs ministries with no National Socialist at their head. The Foreign Office, Economics, Labour, Finance, Justice and Communication ministries report to him, and he is now, virtually, the deputy Führer.

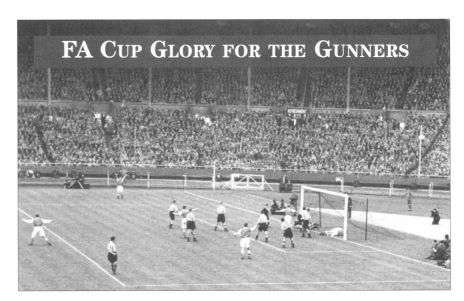

FA CUP GLORY FOR THE GUNNERS

25 Saturday

Arsenal win the FA Cup at Wembley, *above*, beating Sheffield United 1-0.
■ A conference of First and Second Division Football League clubs decides it will not sell the copyright in fixtures. Football pools will be allowed to function without interference.

26 Sunday

Islington puts on a civic reception for the victorious Arsenal team.
■ Italian troops are massing for an attack on Addis Ababa.
■ A new transcontinental **motoring record** is set by Mr T H Wisdom who drove from London, via the north African coast, Cairo and the Syrian desert, to Baghdad in 11 days in a Wolseley light car.
■ A large part of the White Lady Tower at Knaresborough Castle collapses in the moat. No one is hurt. Knaresborough belongs to the King as part of the Duchy of Lancaster.

27 Monday

The committee of Lloyds asks the government if it will hold a special enquiry into the alleged Budget leak.
■ Because she is 58lb heavier than the US

Department of Labour consider she should be, Englishwoman Nora Lee is not allowed to remain in the USA with a view to becoming an American citizen. She weighs 12st 2lbs, and US health charts say that for her age and height she should weigh 8st. Officials say her weight might make it difficult for her to find work, and cite the case of a teacher in New York who was dismissed by the education authorities as she failed to lose enough weight.

28 Tuesday

The Chancellor of the Exchequer Neville Chamberlain promises an enquiry into the alleged budget leak.
■ Crown **Prince Farouk** of Egypt, *left*, a student at the Military Academy in Woolwich, London, becomes king on the death of his father King Fuad. The 16-year-old crown prince will return to Egypt next week. He will govern with a regent.
■ Mrs Anne Sage, the 'woman in red' responsible for the **G-Men**, shooting John Dillinger — America's Public Enemy No. 1 — arrives in New York to await deportation to Romania as 'an undesirable alien', despite having been promised immunity. Mrs Sage has spent the entire £1,000 reward money fighting the deportation order.

■ The Select Committee on the **Civil List** recommend that the King should receive £410,000. But £40,000 will be undrawn while he remains unmarried.

29 Wednesday

After months of careful study, the Jonker diamond— the fourth largest in the world— has been cut into three, from which 12 smaller stones will be cut. The 726 carat stone will lose about 300 carats in cutting and polishing. So great was the risk of shattering the diamond that Lloyds refused to insure the owner, the NY diamond merchant Harry Winston.

30 Thursday

King Farouk leaves London for Marseilles where he will board the P & O liner *Viceroy of India*, which will land him in Alexandria next Tuesday, escorted by the cruiser *Ajax*.
■ A West End store for men only opens on the site of the old Geological Museum in London. It is called **Simpsons of Piccadilly**, and on its nine floors you will be able to buy anything from a hover fly to a light aeroplane.
. . . Poet A E Housman, author of *A Shropshire Lad*, dies in Cambridge at the age of 77. . .

APRIL 29: King Edward VIII sits for his portrait head on coinage and medals. The stamps are released later in the year.

MAY

1 Friday

Sir Herbert Austin (of car fame) gives Cambridge University £250,000 for the extension and further endowment of the Cavendish Laboratories.
■ Moscow stages a magnificent **May Day Parade** with more than 50,000 troops on parade while 700 planes roar overhead.

2 Saturday

John Langley (18), becomes the youngest golfer to enter the finals of the English Golf Championship at Deal, Kent. He is beaten 5 and 4 by Harry Bentley, the Lancashire international and Walker Cup Player, in a close-fought match.
■ Lord Derby's *Tideway* wins the 1,000 Guineas with the King's horse *Feola*, running in Lord Derby's colours, second.
■ **Strawberries** go on sale in May for the first time, grown in the north of Scotland and for sale in Elgin.

3 Sunday

The liner *Queen Mary* escapes harm when fire breaks out at Southampton Docks. Every fireman in the dock and town brigades fights to prevent the fire spreading to the ship.
■ A 76-year old Army pensioner has written to the matron of the Poor Law Institution in Plympton Devon looking for a **bride**. His main condition is that she is at least 70, is

entitled to the 10s per week old age pension and is in ordinary health. He will inspect the likely candidates next week.

4 Monday

Two famous flyers leave today in an attempt to beat Tommy Rose's record flight to Cape Town — Amy Mollison from Gravesend and H L Brook, holder of the Australia-England Light Aeroplane record, from Leeming nr Northallerton.

The *Daily Mail* **is 40 years old today.**

■ Sir Edgar Britten will be the sole captain of the *Queen Mary*. She will not need two captains as she is so easy to handle.

5 Tuesday

Dame Clare Butt, who died in January, leaves £36,717. £3,000 goes to the Royal College of Music for a Clara Butt Fund to help students start on a singing career.

■ The Italian Army enters Addis Ababa. The King of Italy is to be crowned **King of Ethiopia**. Scores of Italian jewellers are searching libraries and museums throughout Europe for details of the Haile Selassie Crown, which Mussolini has ordered them to reproduce.

6 Wednesday
Full Moon

Amy Mollison is in Dahomey. She is more than half way to Cape Town.

■ An ex-miner M Maurice Thorez (Communist), a millionaire, M Leon Blum (Socialist), and an ex-professor, M Edouard Daladier (Radical) will rule **France**.

■ Gold is flooding out of France in the wake of the election. £5 million arrived by air in England yesterday. Holders of gold in France fear that in the event of devaluation of the franc gold will be commandeered. French investors are also selling francs and investing in sterling.

■ **King Fuad** of Egypt is rumoured to have left a fortune of £10 million.

. . . Storms and HEATWAVES across Britain. There are hailstones as big as marbles, thunder and lightning, and the temperature is in the 70's . . .

■ The airship **Hindenburg** sets out on its first voyage across the north Atlantic with 52 passengers, mainly American, German and British, who have been weighed, measured and numbered. Entertainment will be provided by Professor Conrad Wagner, and the ocean concert will be broadcast worldwide.

7 Thursday

The pensioner who wanted a wife from the Plympton Poor Law Institution has found a bride nearer home. He has proposed to a 74-year old widow in a neighbouring village, who has accepted subject to her son's approval.

■ Amy Mollison reclaims her **record** for the flight to Cape Town in 3days 6hrs 26mins. She says she will never make another long solo flight.

8 Friday

The **prehistoric skull** of a young female, 'halfway between the higher apes and man' has been found in Java, where the famous apeman was found in 1891.

■ Scarborough, Yorks, launches its **House Party** scheme, offering free admission to every entertainment and your hotel bill paid up to £4.10s.

■ The *Trail of the Lonesome Pine*, the first picture in colour, starring Sylvia Sidney, Fred MacMurray and Henry Fonda opens at the Carlton Cinema, London, billed as 'the biggest event since sound!'

9 Saturday

The German airship the *Hindenburg*, arrives at Lakehurst, New Jersey, after a 62hr-flight from Frankfurt.

■ **Pierced ears**, usually only seen on Royal ladies or those of a certain age, are all the rage. Trendsetters the Duchess of Kent and the Duchess of Gloucester have both had their ears pierced.

■ **Mussolini** announces the annexation of Abyssinia, and proclaims **Victor Emmanuel II**, *above*, king of both Italy and Abyssinia. The British cruiser *Enterprise* steams into Haifa with the Emperor and Empress of Ethiopia on board. **Haile Selassie** has been offered £20,000 for a fortnight's appearance at an exhibition in Texas, USA, to celebrate its centenary. If he stays a month, they will pay him £30,000.

10 Sunday

Amy Mollison leaves Cape Town at 9.19am in her attempt on Tommy Rose's record for the return flight Cape Town-London.

■ 100,000 people fight to see the *Hindenburg* at Lakehurst, New Jersey. Nine men and a woman are crushed and seriously injured. **G-Men** and New York detectives mingle with the crowd in case of anti-Nazi sabotage.

■ A battalion of the Royal Scots Fusiliers and light tanks from Egypt arrive in **Palestine,** monitoring the increasing tension between Jews and Arabs.

11 Monday

Rabid supporters of Lindbergh baby kidnapper Bruno Hauptmann's innocence swear that there is a **curse on the jury** after a second death. Last February one of the jurors died of a heart attack, and on Friday last another juror was killed by a train.

■ A glass with the figure of **Bonnie Prince Charlie** in highland dress impressed upon it fetches £250 at Christies. Included in the sale was the toast glass from which Sir Joshua Reynolds drank at the Beefsteak Club nearly 200 years ago — the 'steaks' used to drink to 'beef and liberty'.

. . . UNEMPLOYMENT fell by 50,301 to 1,831230 in April . . .

12 Tuesday

Amy Mollison spent last night in Mpika— 200 miles north of Broken Hill, N Rhodesia. She hopes to be back in Britain on Thursday.

■ Mr J H Thomas, the Colonial Secretary, and his son Leslie Thomas, a partner in a Stock Exchange firm, may be connected with the **Budget leak**.

■ Italy walks out of the **League of Nations** Council because the Ethiopian delegate is allowed to attend.

■ The *Queen Mary* is officially handed over from shipbuilders John Brown Ltd to owners Cunard White Star.

13 Wednesday

Doris Carter, Australian high jumper, receives confirmation of her inclusion in the **Olympic team** with a request to send her measurements for cream trousers, and that her wardrobe include singlets, trunks and boxing shorts, while Les Harley, Australia's heavyweight boxer, has been asked to provide his measurements for a white dress!
■ The **Hindenburg** is seen over Gloucester at 10.30pm. Crowds rush out into the street to see it. It is the first airship to make the double crossing of the Atlantic since the R100 in 1930.

14 Thursday

Amy Mollison leaves Athens at dawn, but is **forced down** in Graz, Austria, because of bad weather in the Alps.
. . . The Queen Mary makes a 24-hour cruise from Southampton. . .

15 Friday

Amy Mollison arrives back in Britain at 1.35pm having made the return flight from Cape Town in 4days 16hrs and 17mins. She is greeted by an enthusiastic crowd at Croydon and reclaims her record having made the flight London-Cape Town-London in 12 days 15hrs.
■ Mr Geoffrey Lloyd, Under Secretary for Home Affairs says that no fewer than 30 million **gas masks** are to be produced for British civilians.
■ Britons are invited to subscribe to two schemes adopted by the King George V **National Memorial Fund:**
1. National Playing Fields and, 2. A statue of the King in Abingdon Street, Westminster.

16 Saturday

Hundreds of childless couples make a **pilgrimage** to Callander, Ontario, the home of the Dionne quintuplets, to pick up a 'magic pebble'. The quins' physician says he gets many letters, some including money and that couples who take away pebbles often come back for a visit with their babies.

17 Sunday

The **hottest** Sunday of the year. Temperature reaches 71°F in London and 80°F in Tunbridge Wells.
■ The Russian cargo steamer *Ussuri* hits a wood groyne at Seaford, Sussex, rides up the shingle beach and bores into the stonework of the promenade. She is finally refloated 13hrs later.

18 Monday

The **BBC** appoints its first women announcers — **Jasmine Bligh**, *below*, and Elizabeth Cowell.
■ **Prince Aly Khan** marries Mrs Joan Guinness (formerly the Hon Joan Yarde Buller) in Paris.
■ **Mussolini** is seeking an injunction on *A Night at the Opera*, to prevent the film being shown in Europe.
. . . Britain's SMALLEST BABY, Mary Rose Legg of Swindon, Wilts, is fed every 90 mins with a fountain pen filler. She weighs just 18ozs, and is making excellent progress.

19 Tuesday

The King tours the **Chelsea Flower Show** wearing a straw hat for the first time since he ascended the throne. If the fine weather continues, hatters anticipate a boom year.

20 Wednesday
New Moon

King Leopold of the Belgians

MAN BEHIND THE BUDGET LEAK

THE COLONIAL SECRETARY, J H Thomas, resigns his office and from Parliament after it is revealed that he was paid an advance of £20,000 for his life story by Alfred Bates – the man at the centre of the Budget Leak Enquiry – £15,000 of which was spent on a house and deducted from the advance. The final blow is the sensational disclosure by one of the witnesses at the enquiry, Dr R J Hearn, that he was told by a friend he had 'ways and means of getting information from a member of the Cabinet', and mentioned J H Thomas.

flies to England on a **secret mission** — his third sudden and secret visit in six months.
■ A proposal to admit women undergraduates as debating members of the **Oxford Union** is defeated by 301-169 votes.

21 Thursday

Fruit growers throughout the country light paraffin flares and keep vigil over precious crops as the temperature falls towards danger point.
■ The Postmaster General reveals three improvements to be introduced into service. 1. Emergency calls: dials will be engraved with a simple unusual number that when dialled will light a special lamp and ring an alarm bell at the exchange. 2. A mobile post office which can be utilised at agricultural shows, etc. is now under construction. 3. Readily accessible special enquiry bureaux to open soon.

22 Friday

Colonial Secretary James H Thomas **resigns** from the government (see panel).

■ **Eton College** offers its playing and practice pitches to local elementary schools to encourage the game of cricket. Several hundred boys will play there this summer coached by George Hirst, the former England and Yorkshire cricketer.
... **The Marx Brothers' film** *A Night at the Opera* opens in New York...

23 Saturday

Confirmed **drug addicts** in Britain now number 30,000 according to figures produced by the Opium Section of the League of Nations.
■ Police are called to a **clash** between Sir Oswald Mosley's bodyguards and undergraduates at a Fascist Rally in the Carfax Rooms, Oxford.

24 Sunday

The Open Air Theatre in Regents Park, London is under pressure and needs £5,000 to survive. The founder/director Sydney Carroll has so far sunk £10,000 into the enterprise and feels unable to risk more. His profit last year was £5.

■ **Derby Sunday:** Fortune-tellers and fair operatives enjoy what may be the last Derby Sunday, when the public are free to wander over the famous racecourse. Stewards complain that too much damage is done for the tradition to be allowed to continue.

25 Monday

Continued unrest in **Palestine**. Arabs cut power and telegraph lines at Gaza. British families take shelter in the police barracks.
■ The King, Queen Mary, the Duke and Duchess of York, the Duke and Duchess of Kent and the Duchess of Gloucester tour the *Queen Mary* at Southampton.
■ The original manuscript of *The Old Wives Tale* by Arnold Bennett is sold at Sotheby's for £1,250, considerably less than was expected.
■ The **Everest** climbers are racing the monsoon, and there are fears that the heavy snow fall that follows the monsoon may ruin the chances of Hugh Ruttledge's expedition.

26 Tuesday

Queen Mary is 69 today. She will move into Marlborough House (one of the few examples of Christopher Wren's domestic architecture) in the autumn. The liner Queen Mary is dressed overall in her honour.

27 Wednesday

The *Queen Mary*, sets sail on her **maiden voyage** (see pages 46-47).

■ **Derby Day**: The Aga Khan wins the Derby for the third time with **Mahmoud** (100-8), ridden by Charlie Smirke by three lengths from his other horse **Taj Akbar** (6-1) ridden by Gordon Richards.
. . . BULLION: $4,100,000 in gold shipped from France to New York . . .

28 Thursday

12 noon: The *Queen Mary* has completed 326 miles at an average speed of 28.73 knots. She left Cherbourg at 12.32 this afternoon (ship's time). New York plans a splendid welcome, and the progress of the liner is watched with as keen interest in the USA as in Britain.
■ The **Dionne Quins** celebrate their 2nd birthday at Callander. Mr Croll of the Department of Public Welfare presents the guardians with a cheque for $1,000 (£200). The guardians have signed a contract for three films starring the Quins for $50,000.
■ Princess Assah, elder sister of the King of Iraq, marries Anastassios Haralamides — a waiter who acted as a guide to the princess during her recent stay on Rhodes.

29 Friday

A **stowaway** is found in the engineers' quarters on the *Queen Mary* — Frank Gardener (41) of Cardiff. A builder's labourer, he has been out of work for seven months and is hoping to find a job in the USA. By noon today the ship has covered 747 nautical miles at an average speed of 29.88 knots in the last 24 hours.
■ The King's **Coronation** is proclaimed, *left,* at 10am as tradition demands at St James's Palace, Charing Cross, Chancery Lane and the Royal Exchange.
■ The **Oaks** is won by Sir Abe Bailey's **Lovely**

MAIDEN VOYAGE TRIUMPH

THE QUEEN MARY

BUILT: John Brown Shipyard, Clyde.
LAUNCHED: February 14, 1936. **TONNAGE:** 80,733.
CAPACITY: Max. 1,840 passengers; Fares from £37 5s.
AVE. SPEED: 31 knots.

MAY 27

The super liner Queen Mary leaves Southampton on her maiden voyage. She will reach New York in four days, sailing at an average speed of 31 knots. Thousands of people throng Southampton Dock to witness her departure, and gaily decorated pleasure boats, steamers and small craft escort her for several miles. On the voyage, the shops on 'Burlington Arcade' do a roaring trade, and within two days of her departure, only 900 of the 20,000 postcards on board remain. There are 20 broadcasters on board, 9 British, 8 American, one French, one Dutch and a Dane, using 22 BBC microphones. With an average daily population of 3,000, there are nearly 400 foodstuffs stored on board. In a year, the ship will require 40,000lbs of fish, 42,000 gallons of milk, 725,000 bottles of beer and, appropriately, 20,000 bottles of champagne . . .

OF A VERY SPECIAL LADY ...

Rosa (33-1) by ¾ of a length from Sir Fred Eley's *Barrowby Gem* and the King's *Feola* (running in Lord Derby's colours).

30 Saturday

Dr Julian Huxley opens **Pets Corner** at London Zoo. You can meet George the penguin, three little pigs, Larry the lamb, rabbits, goats, one llama, an ordinary parrot, a pair of talking cockatoos, Nameless the Tortoise (50), George the camel, Percy the python and Jackie the chimp. Along one side are the Untouchables, animals too strong or too wild for children to pet.

■ 12 noon: The *Queen Mary* has covered 766 miles in the last 24 hours at an average speed of 30.6 knots (the world record for a full day's run on the western course).

■ **Fred Perry** (GB) beats C. Boussos (Fr) in the semi-finals of the French Tennis Championship in Paris, and will meet Gottfried von Cramm in the final on Monday.

31 Sunday

Union Day, South Africa

Whitsun: it's one of the coldest for many years.

■ **President Roosevelt** attends the Memorial Day ceremony at Arlington Cemetary, Washington, at which 10,385 veterans (ranging in age from 89-95) of the American Civil War are present.

■ The **Emperor of Ethiopia,** with his two sons and daughter, leaves Gibraltar for the UK.

■ The *Queen Mary* is **delayed** by thick fog for 12 hours. At noon today she has covered a total distance of 2,517 sea miles at an average speed of 29.15 knots.

JUNE

1 Monday

Whit Monday: Weather dry and chilly
The last stages of the **maiden voyage** of the *Queen Mary, above,* are broadcast. She berths at 4pm in New York. At 9.03am she passes the Ambrose Light having crossed in four days 12hrs 24mins. Fog robs her of the record crossing. She is escorted in by clouds of aeroplanes and shoals of smaller ships to a deafening noise. As the ship passes up river, the passengers can see people standing on every available roof halfway across Manhattan and on the New Jersey banks training their field glasses on the ship. The Battery is packed; sirens and whistles blow, bells are rung and the fireboats play jets of water. Broadway stages a tickertape welcome. The pride of the Cunard fleet has a new pier at West 50th Street.

■ Italy approves the constitution of Italian East Africa. The country will be governed by a Viceroy, a Governor General and five subsidiary divisional governors.

. . . TENNIS: At the French Championships, Fred Perry is beaten by von Cramm in the men's singles, and the women's title is won by Fr S. Sperling (Den) after a long – and boring – baseline battle . . .

2 Tuesday

A daring new form of **robbery** in the USA. Two bank officials are robbed of $50,000 from their car when they stop at traffic lights. The robbers draw alongside flourishing guns, and order them to surrender the money.

■ Sir Percy Bates, chairman of Cunard and Capt Sir Edgar Britten call on Mayor La Guardia in New York. **Visitors** will be allowed on board the *Queen Mary* for four hours a day for a $1 charge. The fee will go to the Seamen's Fund.

3 Wednesday

Emperor **Haile Selassie**, arrives in London from Gibraltar. His two sons are pictured *right*.

■ Chipperfield Common, Kings Langley, Herts, 113 acres of woods and heath, is presented to Hemel Hempstead Rural District Council by the Blackwell family.

■ 300 factories in Paris are closed with sit-ins. 300,000 workers are on strike.

■ Thousands of New Yorkers brave intense heat to visit the *Queen Mary*. Sir Percy Bates (the chairman of Cunard) and the British ambassador to the USA are received by President Roosevelt at the White House.

4 Thursday

Rumours are circulating on Clydeside that the government has decided to advance £500,000 for the construction of a sister ship for the *Queen Mary*.

■ **Conscription** in Austria, after 18 years. The 15,000 men born in 1915 are ordered to report to recruiting offices.

. . . SNOW in Switzerland blocks the Alpine passes to vehicular traffic. . .

■ Socialist Leon Blum becomes premier of France when the Popular Front of Left Wing parties wins the election.

5 Friday
Full Moon

The Burgomeisters and Corporation of **Ypres** decide to name one of their streets Avenue Kipling in honour of the writer who died recently.

■ Potato growers in Kent, Sussex and Essex are warned to be on the lookout for **Colorado beetle**, which has spread into NE France and Belgium.

■ No newspapers in Paris as **strikes** spread. The employees of the big Paris stores join in.

. . . The *Queen Mary* **leaves New York on her return trip**. . .

6 Saturday

Gatwick Airport is officially opened by Lord Swinton, Secretary of State for Air. It has been used by British Airways for the past month.

■ The *Queen Mary* is again delayed by fog. At noon, after 22 hours, she has covered 621 miles at an average speed of 28.23 knots.

7 Sunday

Queen Mary makes a 23hr run of 679 miles at an average speed of 29.52 knots.

■ It is the 800th anniversary of Melrose Abbey, Roxburghshire. Founded by King David I of Scotland, it was the first Cistercian monastery in Scotland, and the heart of **Robert the Bruce** is alleged to be buried there.

■ Within five days of gaining power, Leon Blum ends the **strikes** which have crippled France. He agrees a 12% pay rise, a 40-hour week, and two weeks' paid holiday per year for all workers.

8 Monday

Tommy Sopwith's new 'J' class yacht **Endeavour II**, *right*, in which he may challenge for the America's Cup, is launched in Gosport, Hants.

. . . The price of bread is reduced by 1/2d. to 7½d for a 4lb loaf . . .

■ Three more books of the **Old Testament** — Judges, Ruth and Esther — have been added by the RNIB to the Braille version of the Revised Version of the Bible.

■ The Ministry of Transport announce traffic improvement schemes including a new **by-pass** for Ashford, Kent, to begin immediately at a cost of £194,000.

■ By noon today the *Queen Mary* has covered 670 miles at an average speed of 29.14 knots and will arrive in Southampton at 3pm on Wednesday.

9 Tuesday

Morris announce a new car, a 14hp six-cylinder saloon — the Morris 14. The fixed head version will sell for £215, the sliding head with safety glass all round for £225.

■ John Birch, a native of Russia who claims to have fought in the Crimean War and who emigrated to Canada in 1866, has just celebrated his 113th birthday in Nipissing Junction, Ontario.

■ Unemployment figures for May show a drop of 126,000 to 1,705,612.

■ The last hansom cab in Glasgow (probably

READY TO CHALLENGE FOR THE AMERICA'S CUP . . .

in Scotland) is sold for £6.5s. at auction.

. . . The *Queen Mary* covers 679 miles at a speed of 29.52 knots.

10 Wednesday

The four largest ships in the world can all be seen in Southampton Docks today. The *Queen Mary* (80,773 tons), *Berengaria* (52,100 tons), *Normandie* (82,799 tons) and *Majestic* (56,000 tons).

■ Because of Court Mourning, the Royal Family will not attend **Ascot** this year.

... The BBC appoints LESLIE MITCHELL as its first male television announcer. He will begin on August 4.

■ Despite the settlement of the strikes in France, many men have still not returned to work, and they have been joined by new strikers from other trades and industries. **Strikes** have now spread to hotels and restaurants.

■ The *Queen Mary* docks at 3.15pm having been delayed once more by fog.

11 Thursday

After 27 years as an MP, Colonial Secretary **JH Thomas** resigns his Cabinet seal.

■ Marshal Badoglio, leader of the Italian Army in Abyssinia, and subsequently Viceroy, has been relieved of office at his own request and Mussolini makes him Duke of Addis Ababa. He will continue as chief of staff.

■ A team of Austrian carrier pigeons, training for the **Olympic Games** with a flight from Regensburg to Vienna, is refused admission to Germany.

12 Friday

The death is announced of M R James, OM , Provost of Eton College and formerly Kings College, Cambridge. M R James is probably best known as a writer of distinction, particularly for his *Ghost Stories of an Antiquary* and *Twelve Medieval Ghost Stories*.

■ The **King** pays a surprise visit to two Ministry of Labour training establishments for young unemployed men, where they are given a course of intensive training in a variety of trades.

■ The LMS railway is experimenting with a weed-killing train. Two tanks containing 7,000 gallons of **weedkiller** spray the track to eliminate the weeds.

13 Saturday

The mayors of Brighton, Hove and Worthing open Shoreham Airport.

■ The Trustees of the British Museum receive the **Evesham Psalter** from the National Arts Collection Fund and manuscripts of A E Housman poems, each written on a single foolscap sheet.

... The USA wins the Wightman Cup by 4 matches to 3, after a sternly fought battle.

14 Sunday

A performance at the Vienna Opera House is brought to a standstill when someone drops a **stink bomb** from the upper gallery. The culprits are thought to be Nazis and that they are demonstrating against the conductor, Bruno Walter, who had to leave Germany because of his Jewish descent.

■ Settlements of the strikes in Paris. Workers will return to work tomorrow.

■ Heavy rain. Over an inch at Skegness, and Wallasay, Cheshire.

... The death is announced at his home in Beaconsfield of G K CHESTERTON (62), poet, novelist, critic and debater, best known for his fictional detective Father Brown. . .

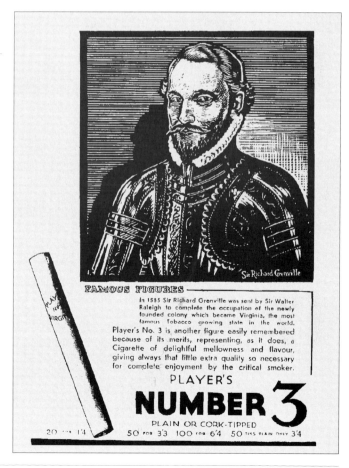

■ A stream of cars, special coach trips from London and even a motorcoach packed with trippers from York pour into Ferring, Sussex (see page 44), to see the £15,000 house of the former Colonial Secretary J H Thomas.

15 Monday

The staffs of the big Paris stores are still sitting-in on strike.

. . . Britain abandons SANCTIONS against Italy.

■ The **Wellington Bomber,** *right,* makes its first flight.

■ The **Imperial War Museum** has moved to its new home— the old Bethlehem Royal Hospital, Lambeth, and will be opened on July 7 by the Duke and Duchess of York.

. . . The King pays a surprise visit to ASCOT Racecourse to view the recent improvements.

16 Tuesday

Opening of Ascot Races. Two girls cause a stir by appearing without stockings, and with their toenails painted to match their finger nails.

■ The London Gliding Club at Dunstable, Beds, offers a two-week **gliding** course for 40 people — no women — for a fee of £11.15s.

■ A meeting of the National Federation of Retail Newsagents, Booksellers and Stationers passes a resolution that the present extensive broadcasting of news has an adverse effect on the sale of newspapers.

17 Wednesday

The *Queen Mary* leaves Southampton on her second trip to the USA with a bigger crew. 20,000 people visited the ship while in dock.

■ A special clinic for **hayfever** sufferers is opening this evening at St George's Hospital, Hyde Park Corner. A complete cure for 98% of cases is guaranteed.

■ **Hottest** day of the year. The temperature reaches 76°F in London and 80°F in Herne Bay.

■ **Heinrich Himmler** is appointed head of the Reich's police force.

■ **Heatwave** in Alaska. Temperatures are higher than ever before recorded. At Seward it reaches 108° F and at Fairbanks 85°F.

18 Thursday

The death is announced of the Russian writer **Maxim Gorky**, *below,* (Alexei Maximovitch Pyestokoff) aged 68, one-time rag-picker, errand boy, tramp and dockhand, at Gorky, nr Moscow. In 1932 he returned from exile to Nijni Novgorod, renamed Gorky City.

■ The fastest military aircraft in the world, produced by Vickers for the RAF, makes its appearance at Eastleigh, Hants. It is called the **Spitfire.**

■ Heavy rain at Ascot races, but it dries for *Quashed* to win the Gold Cup beating the American favourite *Omaha* and the French *Bokbul*. She is the first filly to win the Gold Cup for 42 years.

. . . In Paris, COCO CHANEL offers her shop, workrooms and materials to the striking staff and offers to stay as an unpaid consultant, or she will close it down and move to London or New York.

19 Friday
New Moon

The Lord Mayor has received over £90,000 for the King George V Memorial Fund.

■ Mr Chamberlain announces that he agrees in principle with Cunard that a sister ship for the *Queen Mary* should be built. They have already received a tender from John Brown, Ltd, who have the stocks used for the *Queen Mary*. It would mean work for 200,000 men on Clydeside over three years.

. . . Max Schmelling (above) returns home to Germany after knocking out JOE LOUIS (USA) in the 12th round of the World Heavyweight title fight . . .

■ Spectacular storms sweep Britain at midnight: a **whirlwind** at Deal blows a boat onto the seafront 30 yards up a hill, and a pigeon flying over a house in Maidenhead falls with its wings in flames.

■ There is a total **eclipse** of the sun, observable from Greece to Japan, at 3.01 GMT.

20 Saturday

The continuing **drought** in the USA threatens crops. More than 40 million bushels of spring wheat have been lost since the beginning of the month.

■ Building Societies Assocation is formed.

■ After a trial flying lesson, the wife of the famous airman Mr H L Brook decides she will learn to fly so that she can help him in an attempt on the England-Cape Town **record** held by Amy Mollison.

21 Sunday

Third night of **storms**. All northbound trains from Kings Cross are diverted through Hertford as part of the embankment between Harpenden and St Albans is washed away. St Albans Abbey is struck by lightning, walls collapse in Manchester, and the BBC regional programmes are off the air for 45 min. A crowd sheltering in a garage at Brentwood are horrified when the roof, weighing a ton, is ripped off and flung 70ft. Three seconds later lightning strikes the garage again.

■ Dinard, Brittany, commemorates the 100th anniversary of the first Briton who went to live there, and the principal street is renamed Avenue George V.

22 Monday

Opening of the **Wimbledon** Lawn Tennis Championships (see page 55).

■ Lord Burghley, chairman of the Olympic Committee, receives a letter from the Lord Mayor of London offering London as the venue for the **Olympic Games** in 1940.

■ Hundreds watch in horror as an RAF bomber from Gosport **crashes** on the foredeck of the French Lines flagship *Normandie*. Luckily no one is hurt.

■ The airship *Hindenburg*, lands at Lakehurst , New Jersey, USA, completing the crossing from Frankfurt, Germany, in the record time of 61hr 25mins beating the existing record by 32mins.

. . . WINSTON CHURCHILL warns of the state of political paralysis, and expresses surprise that the country does not realise the dangers that face it. . .

23 Tuesday

King Edward VIII's first **Trooping the Colour** ceremony. Queen Mary, is present, dressed entirely in black except for a spray of white orchids. Queen Mary will not attend the garden parties at Buckingham Palace on July 21 and 27. The Duchess of York will be the hostess.

■ Following the disaster with a party of schoolchildren in the Black Forest (see April 18), the LCC Education Committee rules that the teacher/pupil ratio should be changed to two teachers for 40 pupils (instead of 50 pupils), plus an extra teacher per 20 extra children.

24 Wednesday

The RAF goes into action against the Arabs in Palestine for the first time when 70 Palestinian Arabs **ambush** British troops.

■ Almost all of Milton Abbas, Dorset, is included in the sale of Milton Abbey to the Rev John Maillard as a spiritual healing centre.

■ German policemen now have to undergo an annual physical test 'to be worthy to represent the State's authority'. They will be marked on their prowess in track and field, swimming and revolver shooting.

"Tell him to Get Gibbs!"

It's Super-Fatted!

Super-fatting means :—
a richer and more creamy lather — a lather which remains moist — a quick lather in hot or cold water — your face left refreshed and cool. In addition Gibbs Super-Fatted Shaving Cream is surprisingly economical . . . so little goes so far. And it is delightfully perfumed.
CHANGE TO GIBBS TO-DAY.

D. & W. GIBBS, LTD.
Cold Cream Soap Wks.,
London, E.I.

GIBBS SUPER FATTED SHAVING CREAM

GS44T

■ Kelvin Rogers (3) arrives in Philadelphia, USA, from Melbourne, Australia, for an **operation** to remove a nail from his lung. It is said that only Dr Jackson and his new invention, the bronchoscope, can save the boy.

25 Thursday

Mrs H Grosnell of London shocks the London Stock Exchange by becoming the first woman to apply for membership.

■ Buyers come from far and wide for the sale of souvenirs from King George V's famous racing cutter *Britannia*. The 18ft motor launch goes for £300, a boathook fetches £4, and the bunting goes to a country inn in Kent.

■ It takes only 7mins to successfully remove the 3-inch nail from the lung of Kelvin Rogers at Temple University Hospital, Philadelphia.

26 Friday

Mr Frank Parkinson, known as Britain's **shyest millionaire**, offers Leeds University £50,000 to endow scholarships.

■ Mr Arthur Stuart Murdoch, who emigrated from Forres, Scotland to Australia, has left £30,000 to the provost to buy the sole rights in all classes of fishing in the lower portion of the river Findhorn, from the harbour bar to Red Craig, for the residents.

■ US President **Franklin Delano Roosevelt** is chosen by the Democratic Party to run for a second term.

■ The exiled Emperor of Ethiopia, Haile Selassie, arrives in Geneva to address the League of Nations.

27 Saturday

Civil servants in Dublin **revolt** against a Government ban which they allege encroaches upon their personal liberty. Bare arms, legs and open-necked shirts are taboo. The Government says they are unbecoming improper and will not be tolerated.

■ A runaway plane at Liverpool Aeroclub takes off, lifts to 300 feet, circles the airfield four times and crashes in flames. No one is hurt as there was no pilot aboard — he was turning the propeller when the plane just took off.

28 Sunday

The St Neots Quads are **baptized** at Eynesbury Parish Church as arc lights blaze and photographers stand on pews. There is even a microphone hidden in the font.

■ New York has developed plans to protect film stars after **Robert Taylor** is set upon by a frenzied mob of autograph hunters when leaving a cinema on Broadway. A crowd of 1,000 surges towards him and he finds himself lifted above the pavement. He loses his shoes, and a girl snatches the handkerchief from his pocket.

29 Monday

British film star **Googie Withers** (19) is signed up by Douglas Fairbanks Jr to appear in his pictures for the next five years.

■ The BBC's charter is extended for 10 years, and the licence fee is to remain at 10s. per year. 75% of the revenue received from licences goes to the BBC.

■ CRICKET: In the First Test against **India** which started on Saturday, India were all out for 147 runs in the first innings. England's first innings total was 134, and at close of play India have scored 80 for seven in their second innings.

30 Tuesday

Lord Nuffield, *right,* donates £50,000 to St Peter's Hall, Oxford's newest college.

■ By order of the King, the Yeomen of the Guard may shave off their **beards**. Since their formation by Henry VII in 1485, beards have been part of their uniform.

■ Italian delegates to the League of Nations walk out in protest when **Haile Selassie** is allowed to address the League.

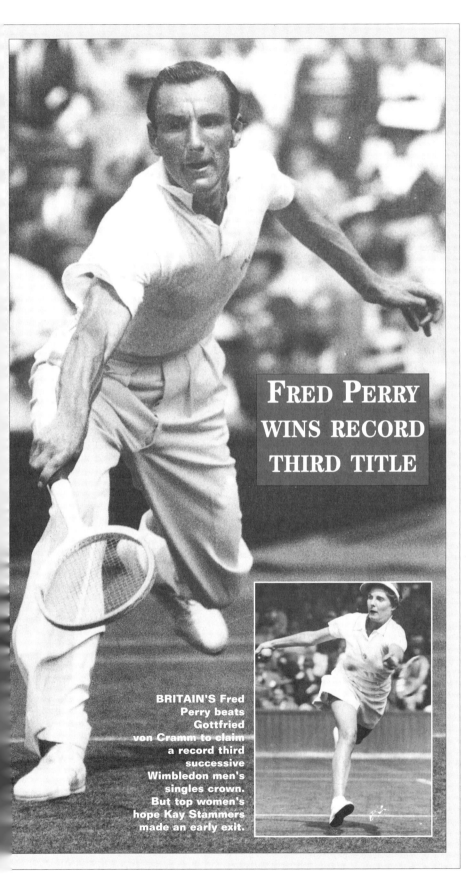

FRED PERRY WINS RECORD THIRD TITLE

BRITAIN'S Fred Perry beats Gottfried von Cramm to claim a record third successive Wimbledon men's singles crown. But top women's hope Kay Stammers made an early exit.

JULY

1 Wednesday
Dominion Day, Canada

The British government intends to develop a great naval and air-force base on the island of Cyprus. It will bring the islanders a prosperity undreamed of since the time of the Romans.

■ Upsets at Wimbledon. British hopes Dorothy Round and Kay Stammers are both beaten in the Women's Singles. Fred Perry will meet Gottfried von Cramm in the Men's Singles final.

CRICKET: England win the First Test against India by nine wickets.

■ Tunbridge Wells Town Council are to poll the residents to decide if **cinemas** should open on Sundays.

■ John Benson and Elisabeth Pantel are **married** 8ft under the water in Puget Sound, Washington State, USA. The bride wears a fetching brown rubber suit with a 30lb helmet, a girdle of lead weights and 30lb shoes.

. . . BOB MARTIN, the dog expert, finds Britain's oldest dog. She is 23 and had her last litter of puppies at 18 . . .

2 Thursday

100,000 families are in need of aid, and 1 million cattle are **starving** to death as the great drought continues in the mid-western states of the USA.

■ Canova's Venus, a 6ft tall white marble statue, is withdrawn from sale at Christie's because no one would pay more than 72gns (another one that couldn't be sold two years ago was

shipped to the USA as ballast).

■ Jane Cain, the Post Office's 'Girl with the Golden Voice' who is the official voice of the talking clock, is to play Celia in *As You Like It* in the Regent's Park Theatre.

3 Friday

Fred Perry of Britain wins his third successive **Wimbledon** singles title beating Baron Gottfried von Cramm of Germany 6-1, 6-1, 6-0. The German pulled a thigh muscle early on and, although in pain, he refused Perry's offer to wait while he had massage and continued the match. After the final, Perry reveals that he has been offered £10,000 to turn professional and go on a four-month exhibition tour of the USA.

4 Saturday
Independence Day, USA

Helen Jacobs (USA) wins the Wimbledon Ladies Singles beating Hilda Sperling (Den). ■ Newest craze in Sydney, Australia, is for **false fingernails**. Non-inflammable, easily applied and waterproof, they come in a box of 10 with a bottle of gum.

■ The curator of the Bournemouth museum reports that two stalactites have formed on one of the pillars of the Pavilion, built just 8yrs ago for £350,000 (stalactites usually take thousands of years to form). He has removed one for display in the museum.

5 Sunday
Full Moon

Although blind, George Themell, a 22-year-old Egyptian born pianist, who taught himself how to play reading Braille with one hand and playing with the other, has won the first prize of the Paris Conservatoire of Music.

■ Large crowds press against the windows of Selfridge's in Oxford Street to see a new type of

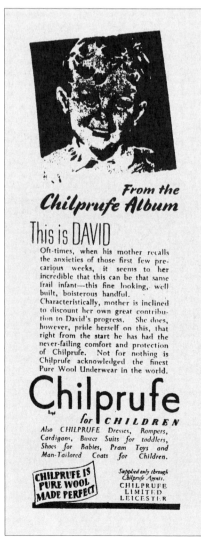

mannequin. Picking up frocks one by one and showing the front and back the mannequin, which is mechanical, can show 34 dresses in 12 minutes.

. . . The League of Nations bars Abyssinia from the League. . .

6 Monday

The Air Minister is considering banning Zeppelin flights over England. Business men and manufacturers believe it is unwise to allow the *Hindenburg* to fly low over northern England. On recent trips she has been able to observe everything that is going on in Barrow, Hull, Leeds, Liverpool, Warrington, Sheffield and Grimsby.

■ **Gold strike** in Wales. 294 tons of ore has been mined from a goldmine in Carmarthenshire once worked by the Romans. 160oz of gold and 150oz of silver have been extracted from the ore.

■ Harry Thompson, a former petty officer in the US Navy, is sentenced to five years' imprisonment for selling **naval secrets** to Japan. His capture exposed a huge international spy ring in the USA.

7 Tuesday

From April 1937, the State will take over the maintenance of all trunk roads from County Councils to bring them up to a uniform standard. One tenth of all the roads in Britain are affected.

. . . Torrential rain sweeps the country. . .

■ The official opening of a lido in Theale, Berks, which has been built over the last four months by typists, housewives and shopgirls in their spare time. Every one of the 40 members of the lido took part. The total cost is less than £50.

8 Wednesday

A violent **explosion** rocks Woolwich Arsenal killing five. It is not sabotage.

■ MPs warn of the dangers of **slimming** by starvation, which can lead to TB.

■ The BBC's Sunday broadcasts are to be brighter. Programmes of dance music will be included, but no jazz.

. . . The King makes an aerial tour of RAF stations in England . . .

9 Thursday

Mr and Mrs Dionne, of **Quins** fame, have a son (their 12th child and 4th son). He will be called Joseph Robert Telesphore, and weighed in at 8lbs.

■ A 29-year-old bank clerk at the Commercial Bank of Scotland, who dared to marry before he earned the regulation

marriage salary of £200 p.a, is sacked. Scottish bank workers threaten demonstrations against the marriage ban.

■ Bella, a guide dog, gives a demonstration organised by the Guide Dogs for the Blind Association to entranced MPs in New Palace Yard, Westminster, She leads a **blind** man through traffic, round corners and up steps in perfect safety.

■ The Prime Minister, **Stanley Baldwin**, *left*, announces an increase of £750,000 to the **dole budget** and an additional £19,600,000 for armaments.

*. . . Non-stop **RAIN** over Britain. 20 million gallons of water falls on Greater London in 24 hours. Hailstones larger than peas stop motor traffic for 15mins nr Woking . . .*

10 Friday

Four new stations for the air force will be built at Linton-on-Ouse, Thistleton, Honington and Swanton Morley.

■ Half of the United States of America is paralyzed by drought. Five million farmers in the Mid West face ruin. President Roosevelt offers immediate government work for 75,000, and promises millions of dollars for relief. Losses in the Mid-West are esti-

-mated to total $60 million. Many areas the size of the United Kingdom are reduced to **deserts of dust**. In South Dakota the temperature reaches 115°F. and it is 100°F in New York.

11 Saturday

Black athlete **Jesse Owens** wins a place in the US team for the Berlin Olympics.

■ Two London men W G Smith of Tooting and V Robinson of Wallington, Surrey, have invented an elecrical apparatus to record the log of an aeroplane. Contained in a small fireproof box it is immediately thrown clear of the wreckage. Mr Smith is employed in the *Daily Mirror* packing department.

... The **STATUE**, below, of St George and the Dragon on the Marylebone War Memorial is judged Best Work of the Year by a British sculptor — Charles Hartwell ...

12 Sunday

Because it is Sunday, Orange Day celebrations in Belfast have been postponed until Monday. All frontiers are being watched to try to prevent gangsters and paid agitators stirring up trouble.

■ **Rainstorms** from Brighton to Plymouth. It is the worst weekend for 10 years.

13 Monday

The eleventh day of the US **heatwave.** It is estimated that about 2,000 have died so far.

■ A police doctor surprises Wolverhampton police court by saying men can do certain things much more capably under the influence of **alcohol** than when sober.

■ 1,000 members of the New York Athletic Club have chartered the *Ile de France*, the second largest liner in the French Transatlantic Line, for a round-trip to the Berlin Olympics. It will also act as an exclusive floating club.

... Spain's monarchist leader Jose Calvo Sotele is MURDERED in Madrid ..

14 Tuesday

Plans for a pageant in Bickham House, Yelverton, Devon on the flight of Charles I from Roundhead soldiers, have aroused the spirit of the king. His **ghost** has been seen several times since rehearsals began.

■ The North American **heatwave** takes its toll in Canada too. In Hamilton, Ontario, the gates of the cemetery are kept open so that burials can go on all night. And in Russia, the heat is burning the crops in the ground.

■ Capt G E Eyston and Albert Denly, smash the 48-hour motor record in *Speed of the Wind* at Salt Lake City. They covered 6,5477.75 miles at an average speed of 136.34mph. The previous record was 5,252 miles at 109.54mph.

15 Wednesday

It could be the **wettest July** on record. Yesterday was London's 11th wet day this month.

■ Mr Anthony Eden is so popular in Norway that a gentleman's summer **suit** has been named

MAN TRIES TO SHOOT KING

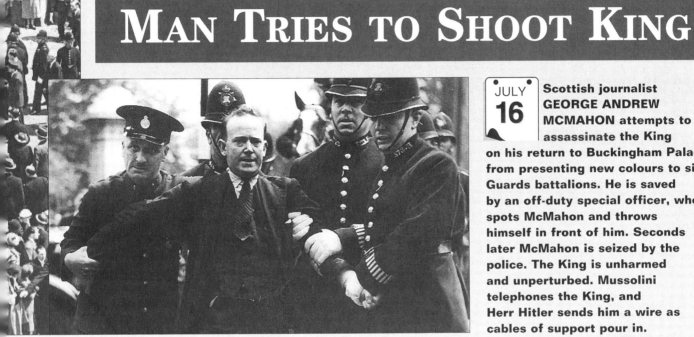

JULY 16 Scottish journalist **GEORGE ANDREW MCMAHON** attempts to assassinate the King on his return to Buckingham Palace from presenting new colours to six Guards battalions. He is saved by an off-duty special officer, who spots McMahon and throws himself in front of him. Seconds later McMahon is seized by the police. The King is unharmed and unperturbed. Mussolini telephones the King, and Herr Hitler sends him a wire as cables of support pour in.

after him — the Eden Kombinasjon.

■ League of Nations lifts **sanctions** on Italy.

16 Thursday

Assassination attempt on King (see panel above)

17 Friday

General Franco leads an **uprising** against the government in Spanish Morocco.

■ **Heinrich Himmler**, head of all the German police, will be appointed minister of Security in the Autumn.

■ Dolls' eyes are included in a long list of articles exempted from Key Industry Duty until August 19. They come under the heading 'lamp-blown glassware'.

18 Saturday

Three changes are announced in the Test team to play **India** at Old Trafford next week.

■ Hand-to-hand fighting between youths and Jewish traders in **Petticoat Lane**, London. Driving up in a lorry, the youths jump out and pull the beard of an elderly Jewish match-

seller. Other traders come to his assistance.

19 Sunday

Gales along the south coast blow treasure trove worth hundreds of pounds to beachcombers as jewellery and money is unearthed.

■ A suburban bookseller has discovered a rare Kilmarnock edition of the poems of Robert Burns published in 1786, in a bundle of books he bought in a furniture shop. It will probably raise £500 at auction,

. . . General Franco arrives in Cadiz at the head of the rebel Spanish foreign legionnaires . . .

20 Monday

The Montreux Conference recognizes Turkish sovereignty of the Dardanelles.

■ Winston Churchill astounds his fellow MPs during the Defence Debate by suggesting a secret session of the Commons to discuss the **emergency** situation. Failing that he would like a private meeting with the Prime Minister about Germany's war preparations and ask questions that could not be asked in the House.

FRANCO TO THE FORE AS SPAIN IS GRIPPED BY CIVIL WAR

THE FALANGIST military revolt in Morocco on July 17, led by Franco, spreads quickly to Spain, supported by monarchists, the Catholic right, landowners and industrialists. A month before the revolt, General Franco wrote to the Spanish War Minister, making it clear that if the Spanish Government could not maintain the normal securities of law in daily life the army would have to intervene. Both sides indulge in wholesale cold-blooded massacres of their opponents. The military cadets defend their college at the Alcazar in Toledo with the utmost tenacity and Franco's troops forcing their way up from the south, finally achieve their relief.

Bottom left: Rebels in the deserted streets of San Sebastian as the government troops fall back to Bilbao. Left: Franco in Burgos where he is declared dictator. Main picture: The ruins of the Alcazar in Toledo after government forces explode the mines. Only one towers remains standing. Bottom: A soldier helps a woman and child to escape from the ruins.

■ Thrown away centuries ago and converted into mummy wrappings, four fragments of a Greek version of the *Book of Deuteronomy*, earlier by 300 years than any other bible manuscript, have been found in papyri in the John Rylands Library, Manchester.

21 Tuesday

Turkey is beflagged to celebrate the signing of the Dardanelles Convention giving her the right to refortify the Straits. She will immediately reoccupy the demilitarized zone. Greece will be free to fortify her islands off the Turkish coast.

■ Buckingham Palace **Garden Party** rained off. Nearly 1,000 women pick up their skirts and run for cover. Only 100 were presented to the King.

22 Wednesday

Battle raging at Addis Ababa between Italian forces and a large Abyssinian army under Ras Kassa.

■ The French Line, owners of the *Normandie*, send a strong appeal for clemency, which is read out at the court martial of Flying Officer Horsey (RN) whose aeroplane crashed on the liner (See June 22).

23 Thursday

Shrapnel fired from Spanish warships tears holes in the roof of the Rock Hotel, Gibraltar.

■ American flyer **Col Charles Lindbergh**, visiting Germany at the invitation of General Goering, arrives in Berlin.

■ The *Queen Mary*, speeding towards New York has covered 476 miles from Cherbourg at an average speed of 29.32 knots.

24 Friday

Reports of **atrocities** committed by the Communists in Barcelona begin to filter out. All the churches in Barcelona are set on fire, Jesuit priests are massacred and nuns stripped and turned out into the streets. The

Fascist Army under Jose Antonio Primo de Rivera, son of the former dictator, is nearing Madrid. The government in Madrid appeals for foreign help in the civil war.

■ George Andrew McMahon (See July 16) appears in Bow Street Police Court and is remanded for a week so that he can call witnesses.

■ British **warships** rescue hundreds of Britons from the storm centres of Spain. *HMS London* is in Barcelona harbour standing by to take off nationals.

25 Saturday

More than 150,000 people converge on Arras for the unveiling by the **King** tomorrow of the Canadian cenotaph at **Vimy Ridge**, *above*. The King leaves Portsmouth on the Admiralty yacht *Enchantress*.

■ **Wally Hammond**, *below*, dominates play in the Second Test at Manchester. India made 203 all out. England replied with 173 for two, Hammond 118 not out.

■ In the Davis Cup final against Australia, **Britain** are two up, Bunny Austin beating Jack Crawford 4-6, 6-3, 6-1, 6-1, and Fred Perry beating A Quist 6-1, 4-6, 7-5, 6-2.

. . . Hitler recognizes Italy's occupation of Abyssinsia.

26 Sunday

The King opens the Canadian **war memorial** at **Vimy Ridge,** *above*. Among the onlookers is one Canadian woman with 21 medals on her coat. Twelve of her sons fought for Canada, and five of them have their names on the memorial.

■ Trouble flares in Danzig when Nazis attack Catholic churches and shrines.

■ The **Olympic flame**, which is being borne by a relay of runners from Olympia in Greece to Berlin, had to be rekindled with a match a few miles past the Yugoslav border.

27 Monday

The King and the Prime Minister, Mr Baldwin, both cancel their holidays in France. The King fears that his visit to Cannes, being so close to Spain, would throw too much responsibility on the French police. And Mr Baldwin feels he should be at hand because of the international situation.

■ Rebel leaders in Spain appeal to Britain, Italy and Germany for help.

■ Although the *Queen Mary* made a record crossing from Cherbourg to New York, she failed by just one hour to wrest the Blue Riband from the *Normandie*.

■ Australia wins the doubles in the **Davis Cup,** while, in the Test, **Wally Hammond** makes 167 in the first innings as England declare at 571-8. India are 190 for no wkt in their second innings.

28 Tuesday

Britain retains the Davis Cup (their 4th successive win). Austin is beaten by Quist, but Fred Perry beats Crawford 6-2, 6-3, 6-3.

■ The German **Zeppelin** Company establishes a mooring station in Belfast so that US passengers can continue to the continent in faster aircraft. An aeroplane from Belfast to Frankfurt takes 4½hrs; Zeppelins around 9hrs.

■ John Brown and Co are to build a sister ship to the *Queen Mary*. Work will begin on No 552 within a month. At 90,000 tons, it will be the world's biggest ship.

■ **Bad light** stops play in the Second Test saving India from defeat.

. . . Torrential rain sweeps much of Britain . . .

29 Wednesday

F G Blandford of Corpus Christi College, an expert on phonetics says there is no such thing as an **Oxford accent**. This fallacy started 30 years ago, and Oxford men have always described it as a Balliol accent. 'As Balliol is primarily a college for Scottish students, I can only suggest that it was an attempt by Scottish undergraduates to introduce some refinement of English pronunciation into their speech, which in time came to be associated with Oxford University as a whole.'
■ The **Olympic torch** was burning too quickly, so the Yugoslav runner carrying it nr Kragujevas was ordered to cycle to the next relay.

30 Thursday

Lord Nuffield gives his 20,000 workers a holiday bonus of £100,000. On Friday night the three works in Cowley, will close for two weeks holiday.
■ The British **Olympic team** sets off for Berlin by train from Victoria.
■ 248,828 calls have been made to the **Speaking Clock** in its first week.
. . . The game MONOPOLY, launched in the USA last year, is the latest craze, selling 20,000 sets a week . . .

31 Friday

Bank Holiday. An estimated 12 million people will head for the sea by rail beween 8am and midnight today, despite bad weather.
■ Men and women competitors are **segregated** at the Olympics. The men live nine miles outside the city, and no women are allowed on the premises. The women are near the stadium, seven miles away.
■ Royal Assent is given to the **Education Bill** which raises the school leaving age to 15, and the Midwives Bill which sets up a national service of salaried midwives.
. . . Last year 4,164 motor vehicles were STOLEN, and 4,052 recovered. . .

AUGUST

1 Saturday

Adolf Hitler opens the **Olympic Games** *above*.
■ For the third year running Peckham Police Station, London, wins the prize for best-kept garden.
■ Scientists from the British Society for Psychical Research are invited to New York to meet Cricket the psychic duck. His owner, Mr Coyne, claims Cricket is controlled by the spirit of Big Moon, an Indian chief.

2 Sunday
Bank Holiday

Heavy rain at most resorts.
■ **Louis Blériot** (64, *right*) the first man to fly across the Channel, dies in Paris.
■ At the Olympic Games in Berlin, **Jesse Owens** (USA) wins his heat in the 100m in a new world record of 10.9sec.

3 Monday
Full Moon

America wins gold and silver in the 100m, **Jesse Owens** taking the gold.
■ Two years ago Bridget O'Farrell (12) of Clonmel, Co Tipperary, was almost blind. She has just been to Lourdes and, after a visit to

the grotto finds she can read even small print.
. . . Frank Whittingham of Lancing, Sussex, breaks the Cross Channel CANOE record in a time of 5hr 50min.

4 Tuesday

Jesse Owens (USA) breaks the **world record** for the 200m and equals it in the second round. In the Long Jump the record is broken six times before Owens wins his second gold.

■ Tommy Sopwith's yacht, *Endeavour II*, will represent the UK in the **America's Cup** challenge sent to the USA yesterday by the Royal Yacht Squadron in Cowes. The races will probably be in July next year.

■ Famous pianist and ex-prime minister of Poland Jan Paderewski (76) arrives in the UK. He is to make the film *Moonlight Sonata*.

5 Wednesday

The Permanent Secretary to the Air Ministry, Sir Christopher Bullock, is dismissed for 'having discussed with Imperial Airways the possibility of becoming a director'.

■ **Jesse Owens** wins the 200m for his third Olympic gold medal. Much favoured **Sidney Wooderson** (GB) fails to qualify for the 1500m final, but **Harold Whitlock**, *right, pictured winning a domestic event,* wins the 5,000m Walk in a new world record time of 4hr 10min. *(See pages 66-67).*

■ The King will set sail in his hired luxury yacht, *Nahlin,* from a Yugoslavian port, accompanied by two naval destroyers, at the start of his holiday – a Mediterranean cruise.

6 Thursday

Leni Reifenstal, star of the film *Blue Light*, is making a film of the Olympic Games. As planes are banned from

overflying the stadium, small balloons carrying cameras sail slowly over the arena. Each camera has a letter asking the finder to return the equipment and film to the stadium.
. . . Mine disaster at Wharncliffe colliery, Yorkshire. 57 pitmen are killed . . .

7 Friday

In Warsaw, Poland, a 25 year-old ex-soldier, who won several medals for bravery, has given birth to a baby. Up to the age of 24, Tenenbaum was a man, but his sex gradually changed. This is believed to be the first time in history that a person who has **changed sex** has given birth to a child.

■ Hugh Ruttledge (51), leader of the unsuccessful Everest expedition, returns to England. He says. 'I am certain that some day it will be climbed.'

8 Saturday

The Foreign Office sends out an SOS to 1,000 Britons still in Spain asking them to contact their nearest consular post if they want to reach safety. 2,000 have already been evacuated by British warships.

■ **Horses** will no longer be allowed in Regent Street, Haymarket, part of New Bond Street, New Oxford Street and High Holborn, London.
. . . Spanish REBELS close the frontier with Gibraltar.

9 Sunday

King Edward VIII arrives in Yugoslavia.

■ Massachusetts Department of Mental Diseases says that divorced men and women show the highest incidence of entry to **mental homes**.

■ Bournemouth Corporation have installed little red honesty boxes inside their trolley buses asking holidaymakers and other passengers to leave their uncollected fares in them during rush hours.

10 Monday

Hundreds of tons of rock and earth block the Southern Railway line at Hooley, cutting the signal wires and blocking the track, following a **cloudburst.**

■ **The King**, *right*, sets out on a cruise of the Adriatic on the hired luxury yacht *Nahlin* with a group of friends, prominent among whom is **Mrs Wallis Simpson**

11 Tuesday

Two **wireless** sets in each home is the slogan for the radio show at Olympia. 289,294 wireless receiving licences were issued in July, a net increase of 23,105 over the previous month.

■ **Joachim von Ribbentrop** is appointed Hitler's ambassador to London. Partly educated in England, his appointment is seen as indicative of the importance Hitler attaches to Anglo-German relations.

12 Wednesday

One of the leaders in the **Baby Marathon**, in which a prize of £10,000 goes to the Toronto, Canada, woman who has the most children in 10 years, has had her 10th child in the stipulated time, which ends on October 31. The prize was the idea of eccentric millionaire sportsman Charles Vance Millar.

■ Construction of the Dartford-Purfleet Tunnel will start within the next few weeks. It will cost £3 million.

. . . Spanish REBELS close the frontier with Gibraltar.

13 Thursday

Fines of 1s. per mile are imposed by Marylebone Police Court. 40mph = £2 and so on. The rates for motor cycles are half.

■ In Spain the rebel forces **bomb** San Sebastian.

■ New York launches the Queen Mary Cocktail. Gin is the base plus fresh lime juice and stone ginger beer, topped with a slice of orange and a cherry.

14 Friday

Jack Beresford and **L F Southwood** win the Double Sculls at the Berlin Olympics. Germany wins five of seven rowing golds.

■ A workman making a dew pond at Whipsnade Zoo is **attacked** by a roebuck. He hangs on to the animal's horns until help arrives. The only damage is to his trousers, and the Zoo promises to replace them.

15 Saturday

The Air Ministry reveals plans to give Britain air supremacy. It is setting up a scheme to extend the reserve of RAF pilots by creating a special category for young men between the ages of 18-25 who are prepared to give 12 months continual attendance for training.

16 Sunday

Sipping cocktails, tourists sit at tables along the river bank at Biriatou on the Franco-Spanish border and watch Spaniards kill each other. Roads are blocked with their cars, and their clothes would grace Ascot.

■ The Berlin Olympics close.

JESSE OWENS STRIKES

THE 1936 OLYMPIC GAMES belong to one man – the legendary American, Jesse Owens. He is a virtual fixture on the winner's rostrum, below, setting a new world record for the 100m of 10.98sec, and going on to win the gold. He then sets a new record in the 200m of 21.7sec, equals it in the second round, and goes on to win the gold medal in a time of 20.7sec. In the long jump, the record is broken six times before he wins the gold medal with a new Olympic record leap of 8.06m. With the US team winning the 4x100m relay, Owens wins his fourth gold medal, and equals the records of J D Lightbody (USA) in 1904 and Paavo (Fin) in 1921.

Nazi newspapers sneer at the 'Black mercenaries' in the US team, and the medals are presented to them in almost total silence, the applause coming only from the foreigners present. Herr Hitler leaves the stadium before he has to meet the black athletes. Britain's medals total four gold, five silver and three bronze. The gold medal winners are: Harold Whitlock, 50km walk; the mens 4 x 400m relay (Frederick Wolff, Godfrey Rampling, William Roberts and Arthur Godfrey Brown); Jack Southwood and L F Beresford (below left), double skulls; and the 6m Class yachting.

GOLD AT BERLIN OLYMPICS

17 Monday
New Moon

Knock, knock jokes sweep New York. A typical example is: Knock, knock. Who's there? Ammonia. Ammonia who? Ammonia bird in a gilded cage.
■ The price of bread goes up by ½d. to 8½d—the highest price for six years.
■ Society woman **Mrs Beryl Markham** (33), is going to attempt to **fly the Atlantic** from East to West. She will take off from Abingdon in her Percival Gull some time this month.
■ Britain's first **flying hospital**, the Red Cross plane *Florence Nightingale*, picks up Vincent Sheean, the American writer and war correspondent, and flies him 900 miles from Dublin to Geneva for treatment.
■ BOXING: Ben Foord (SA) stops Jack Petersen (GB) in the third round to take the British and Empire Heavyweight championships.

18 Tuesday

The official coronation route is announced.
■ The first month of the civil war in Spain has cost 20,000 lives and £125,000.
■ Five men of the US Civil Service arrive in the UK to study public and social service work in Europe. They bring with them a new expression 'boon wiggling', which means employing a man on useless work merely to employ him.

19 Wednesday

The *Queen Mary* is sailing today, with the intention of winning the Blue Riband of the Atlantic.
■ The Moscow Show Trials open. Zinovieff, Leo Kameneff and 14 others are accused of plotting with **Trotsky** to kill Stalin.
■ The death is announced of Spanish writer Federico Garcia Lorca at the age of 37.

20 Thursday

On the first day of her voyage, the *Queen Mary* covers 472 miles at an average speed of 29.5 knots.
■ Because an American woman managed to kiss Adolf Hitler as he was watching the Olympic Games on Saturday, certain members of his personal **bodyguard** have been dismissed or moved to lesser duties.

21 Friday

The *Queen Mary* covers 760 miles at average speed of 30.4 knots.
■ Private aeroplane owners are finding it impossible to fly their planes out of the country because of regulations designed to stop sales of private aircraft to Spain. Owners have had to deposit a sum equal to third of the plane's value with the Royal Aero Club.

22 Saturday

The GPO have recruited S-Men to solve postal puzzles. Handwriting illegible to even expert sorters, hieroglyphics, Hindustani, Persian, Russian and Greek script all come within the S-Men's province.

23 Sunday

The **BBC** shows its first demonstration TV programme at Alexandra Palace.
■ The death of **Sir Thomas Cullinan** (74) famed for the **Cullinan diamond**, *above*, in the Crown Jewels. He was the discoverer and chairman of Premier Diamond Mines in South Africa when the diamond was found in 1907.

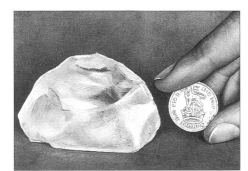

24 Monday

Kaye Midwinter of Torquay, completes a three-day journey on **horseback** across the Alps from Geneva to Berne. It has never been done before. Miss Midwinter works at the League of Nations Secretariat in Geneva.
■ Donald Sullivan (23) of Lydney, Gloucs, swims the river Severn from Sharpness Docks to Lydney — two miles from bank to bank — in 43 min. The changing currents have always defeated earlier attempts.
■ The 16 defendants in the Moscow Show Trials are **sentenced** to death.
. . . The temperature in London is 82°F in the shade. .

25 Tuesday

With the Blue Riband of the Atlantic within her grasp the *Queen Mary* runs into her old adversary — fog — on the last lap.
■ Representatives of **Marlene Dietrich** pay £60 for bed-linen belonging to the late John Gilbert, whose household effects are auctioned in Hollywood today. The actor's daughter Leatrice Joy (11), puts up a spirited fight for as many of her father's possessions as she can afford.
■ In Moscow, Zinovieff, Kameneff and 14 others are executed.

26 Wednesday

The father of a fat son (the boy is four and weighs 12 stone) who is fined 10s. for employing the boy and 10s. for causing him to take part in an entertainment, says he was refused free food tickets and told by the Lowestoft Public Assistance Committee that he should put the boy on show.
■ Spanish **rebels** occupy the Rio Tinto copper and sulphur mines in southern Spain.
■ The Post Office reveal the design of the new Edward VIII ½d, 1½d and 2½d. **stamps** which will go on sale on Tuesday.

27 Thursday

At the court martial of Flying Officer Horsey, the pilot who crash landed on the *Normandie* (see July 22), he is severely reprimanded and sentenced 'to take rank and preference as if appointed Flying Officer July 21, 1936'.
■ The *Queen Mary* begins a fresh bid for the Blue Riband. She covers 580 miles at an average speed of 30.13 knots.
■ The eldest son of ex-King Alfonso of Spain is rushed into hospital in New York, when he again falls victim to **haemophilia.**

JANE'S JOURNAL—The Diary of a Bright Young Thing - - - - - - *No Insects!*

DECIDED A LITTLE ADVERTISEMENT WOULDN'T DO ANY HARM, SO PUT UP A BOARD.

I SOON GOT A CAT FOR TREATMENT

AND A DOG — BUT WAS NONPLUSSED BY ONE SPECIMEN WHO SAID

HIS WIFE HAD SENT HIM TO BE LOOKED AFTER!

ALL KINDS OF ANIMALS CARED FOR

28 Friday

Purge in Russia. The Norwegian Minister of Justice interns Leon **Trotsky** and his wife. Two of his secretaries are expelled.
■ SIT-IN: 64 **miners** stay in at Fernhill Colliery, Treherbert, Glam. They refuse to come up until management pay the money alleged to be due to 12 of their number under the Minimum Wage Statutory Act.
■ **Derbyshire** wins the County Cricket Championship for the first time in 62yrs.
■ **Randolph Scott**, supposedly one of Hollywood's confirmed bachelors, secretly married an old school friend, divorced society woman Mrs Marion du Pont Somerville, in Charlotte, North Carolina on March 23.

29 Saturday

King Carol of Rumania finally ends his long-standing relationship with Mme Lupescu. She is said to be receiving £1million, as well as a villa on the French Riviera.
. . . Norway refuses request from the Soviet government to DEPORT Leon Trotsky. . .

30 Sunday

The *Queen Mary* wins the **Blue Riband** of the Atlantic for Britain for the first time since the *Mauretania* lost it to the *Bremen* in 1929, with a record crossing of 3days 23hr and 57min to the Bishop Rock, Scilly Isles from Ambrose Light, New York. She knocks 31min off the record set by the French liner *Normandie,* last June. The *Queen Mary* made the double crossing in just 11 days.
■ The BBC's **first television broadcast** is relayed to the Radio Exhibition at Olympia, where 5,000 people queue to watch. **Leslie Mitchell**, *right,* makes his debut as announcer. The programme shows excerpts from new films including Paul Robeson in *Showboat,* and Charles Laughton and

Gertrude Lawrence in *Rembrandt*. Also showing is a documentary presented by A P Herbert and Julian Huxley on the history of writing from cave drawings to newspapers. New **television sets** will be on sale for about 100gns and measure just 10in x 8in.

31 Monday

Crowds of viewers at Radiolympia, Waterloo Station, the Crystal Palace and the Baird Theatre, Haymarket, see the *Queen Mary* arrive in Southampton.
■ Leon Trotsky is given permission to stay in Norway, but he will be kept **under guard** and not allowed to use the telephone.
■ It has been the **driest** August for years. Only 1.2mm of rain fell during the entire month. It is 82°F at Dawlish, Devon.
■ **Wally Hammond** hits **317** for Gloucestershire against Notts in 6½hr, beating W G Grace's record for the most runs scored in a month.

SEPTEMBER

1 Tuesday
Full Moon

The first **King Edward VIII stamps** go on sale. 30million are sold in the first 24hr (see page 40).
■ Charles Mason of Dover, sets out on an air mattress to paddle across the Channel using only his hands. It takes him 5hr 46min to cover the 13½ miles to the East Goodwin Lightship, where he decides to give up.
■ Canada's Dionne **Quins** have had more than 140,000 visitors to their home in Callander, who have arrived in 67 buses and 30,216 cars. There is free parking, a souvenir shop and a clock that tells you when the Quins will next be on view.

2 Wednesday

The Great Ziegfield starring William Powell, Luise Rainer, Myrna Loy and Billie Burke, opens in London. It is the longest talking film ever made (three hours), and is shown in two parts with an interval.

■ **Dick Merrill** and **Harry Richman**, *right,* take off from Floyd Bennett Field, New York, on their sub-stratosphere flight to London and back, which they hope to accomplish in 32 hours. Their monoplane has oxygen tanks, a wireless and 40,000 ping-pong balls in the wings to ensure buoyancy.

■ Britain's **Walker Cup** golfers at Pine Valley, New Jersey, make a bad start. The USA wins the foursomes 2-0 with two halved.

3 Thursday

The *Queen Mary* is to have her funnels made taller to get rid of the smoke and smuts that currently make life uncomfortable for passengers on the tourist deck.

■ **GOLF:** USA wins the Walker Cup 9-0.

■ A second sit-in **strike** at Bedwas Mine. Unless something happens in the next 48 hours, 120,000 Welsh miners will strike.

4 Friday

Harry Richman and **Dick Merrill** land in a farm field in Carmarthenshire, Wales, having flown from New York in a new record time of 18hr 8min at an average speed of 210mph and at a height of 11,000ft. They passed Ireland without seeing it and circle 90min trying to get their bearings before lack of fuel forces them to land.

■ Despite the threat of gales, **Beryl Markham** (31), the society lady pilot, takes off from Abingdon to **fly the Atlantic** solo. She has chicken sandwiches, dried bananas, raisins, black coffee, tea and brandy but no wireless.

■ King Edward VIII receives a rapturous welcome in **Turkey.**

5 Saturday

The **auction** of John Gilbert's household treasures raised a total of £70,000.

■ Britain calls up 3,000 Army **reserves** and

sends a further 12,000 troops to Palestine.

. . . The MINERS' UNION orders pits to get ready for a general stoppage. . .

6 Sunday

The British Ambassador in **Madrid** tells the 130 Britons still remaining in the city that the rebels may drop **mustard gas**.

■ Beryl Markham is cheered by a crowd of 5,000 when she alights from her plane in New York. She was forced down on Cape Breton Is., Nova Scotia, through lack of fuel, and was flown to Halifax before flying on to New York. She makes the first Atlantic crossing east to west (Ireland to Newfoundland) by a woman in 16½ hr.

■ **The King** leaves Turkey to return home overland, travelling in Kemal Ataturk's special train. He will stop in Bulgaria to meet King Boris before continuing to Vienna.

7 Monday

The stay-in strikers at Ferndown Colliery have been down 230 hours — a record.

■ Sir John Cadman, chairman of the Anglo-Persian Oil Co. speaking at the World Power Conference in New York, says that the world's supply of **oil** will last only another 20 years and we must develop a new type of motor fuel from natural gas and coal.

8 Tuesday

Society ladies and government officials bombard the **Old Bailey**, London, for seats at the trial of **George McMahon**, (see July 16) which will begin on September 14.
■ Master criminal James Wilson (83), former wealthy racehorseowner and forger, is sentenced to three years penal servitude at the Old Bailey. His **forgeries** were so good the Bank of England was forced to change their designs.
■ The engagement is announced between **Princess Juliana** of the Netherlands and **Prince Bernhard** zur Lippe Biesterfeld, *right*.

9 Wednesday

Security alert in Vienna when two **bombs** explode in the railway station. King Edward VIII is expected to stay in Vienna until Saturday.
■ An RAF **pilot escapes** with cuts and bruises when his plane crashes on the main railway line 10 miles north of Crewe just seconds before the Manchester-London express roars through, and just after the London-Carlisle express passed. The rail is inches clear of the plane.
■ John Cobb, the racing motorist, sets **four new speed records** for Britain at the Bonneville Salt Flats, Utah, USA: the 100km at 167.618mph; the 100 miles at 168.89mph; the 200km at 168.266mph and the hour at 167.69mph.
■ The **St Leger** is won by the 20-1 outsider *Boswell* ridden by Pat Beasley. The Aga Khan's *Mahmoud* is third.

10 Thursday

A new British **invention** catches the eye at the Wine and Beer Trade Exhibition at Grosvenor House, London— a device for putting a head on draught beer.
■ Queen Ena of Spain dashes 3,000 miles to the bedside of her son the Count of Covadonga suffering from **haemophilia** in hospital in New York. He has had eight blood transfusions in the last fortnight.

11 Friday

While 200 people are dining in the restaurant at Wembley Stadium, **thieves** steal the Greyhound St Leger Gold Cup from a glass case in the restaurant and get away.
■ The maiden flight of the Caledonia — the first long-range **flying boat** adapted for Atlantic service.
. . . Helen Jacobs (USA) beats Kay Stammers, Britain's last hope in the women's singles at the US tennis Championships 6-4, 6-3. . .

12 Saturday

The MCC team leave Southampton for Australia hoping to bring back the **Ashes.**
■ **Fred Perry** (GB) beats Donald Budge (USA), 2-6, 6-2, 8-6, 1-6, 10-8, in the final of the Men's Singles at the US Championships. Perry also won the title in 1933 and 1934, so his third win means the trophy is his own, the first time a foreigner has achieved this.

13 Sunday

Thousands of **cheering** people wave King Edward VIII off from Vienna.
■ Birmingham Corporation used to use a fleet of cars to carry councillors to meetings up to 100 miles away. But as separate cars mean that the councillors cannot exchange views until their return, and traffic congestion in the streets causes delay, the Corporation has commissioned a motor coach with an interior like a municipal boardroom for councillors.

14 Monday

George Andrew McMahon is sentenced to 12 months hard labour for producing a pistol with intent to kill the king (see July 16).
■ Charles Laughton, who is starring in *Mutiny on the Bounty*, was walking down Bond Street when he saw the name Gieves. He recalled seeing the name in Captain Bligh's biography, and popped in to ask them if they made Bligh's uniforms. They turned up the original 150-year-old patterns, so Laughton ordered a duplicate wardrobe.

15 Tuesday
New Moon

American pilots Richman and Merrill (see September 2) leave Southport, Lancs, at 3.03am and come down at Musgrave Harbour, nr Bona Vista, Newfoundland at 8.47pm crossing the Atlantic in 17hr 44min. It is the first return crossing to be achieved.
■ Thousands of **hop pickers** are leaving

Kent, driven away by the bad weather, the tally which regulates wages, and the very small size of the hops.
■ George Andrew McMahon is to **appeal** against his sentence.
■ Opening of the **Empire Exhibition** in Johannesburg, South Africa to commemorate the jubilee of the city.

16 Wednesday

The Post Office Savings Bank reveals that one person in four has money in POSB— they have 10 million active account holders.
■ **Sarah Churchill** (23) leaves a note for

her parents saying she is going to the USA and her engagement to comedian **Vic Oliver** may be announced soon. She sails in the *Bremen*. Her brother Randolph follows her 23 hours later in the *Queen Mary*.

17 Thursday

Tweed evening coats that open to show lapels lined with gold kid or velvet embroidered with brilliantly coloured beads are the big news from Schiaparelli. Skirts are short, narrow, flat and slit with zip fasteners.
■ Leslie Wood, a London film writer, bought a few feet of **film** from a secondhand dealer in Brighton for sixpence. It was the original of one of the earliest films ever made, the *Boat Race of 1895*, and is part of the collection he is presenting to the Museum of Modern Art in New York.

18 Friday

The executors of Charles Vance Millar, the sponsor of the Toronto Baby Marathon, decide to throw open the competition by allowing **unmarried mothers** to take part. Mrs Matthew Kenny, with 12 children, is the apparent leader, but may be disqualified as

not all of the children have been registered.
■ The Earl of Warwick signs a seven-year film contract with MGM, which will eventually bring him £40,000 p.a.
. . . The Alcazar Citadel in Toledo is blown up. . .

19 Saturday

Leonard Phillips (22) and Gloria Feori (25), set out to cross the Channel on water skis. They hope to cross in 50min.
■ Crooner and film star Dick Powell **marries** fellow film star Joan Blondel on board the liner *Santa Paula* in Wilmington Dock, San Pedro, California.
■ British authors and composers have formed a union, the British Authors' and Composers' Protection Association, to further the interests of popular song writing and push for more exposure on the BBC — at least 40% of the music played.

20 Sunday

Chaperoned by Lady Astor and a New York lawyer, Sarah Churchill and Vic Oliver meet when the *Bremen* docks (see September 16). Broadway is bewildered, as only yesterday Vic Oliver was saying an engagement was out of the question. Randolph Churchill arrives tomorrow.
■ There is a four-mile traffic jam around **Balmoral** as hundreds of people crowd in to see the King go to church at Crathie — his first service in Scotland as a Presbyterian since he came to the throne. The King and his brothers wear the light grey Balmoral tartan.

21 Monday

Sarah Churchill may have permission to marry Vic Oliver as a result of a two hour conference with her brother Randolph.
■ The death is announced of **Frank Hornby** (73), the inventor of **Meccano,** the marvellously accurate clockwork and electric Hornby trains, and Dinky toys. In later life, he took up politics, and for a time was Conservative MP for the Everton Division of Liverpool.

22 Tuesday

Gangsters are threatening the mothers in the Toronto Baby Marathon. One mother has received a phone call saying, 'Unless you settle with certain persons you won't live to touch any of the money'.
■ British troops are pouring into **Palestine** as the bombing continues.
. . . A girl from Indiana who smashed into CLARK GABLE's $28,000 roadster, made him scratch his autograph on her paintwork . . .

23 Wednesday

17 are killed and 30 injured when a train from Lourdes, full of pilgrims, is smashed to pieces by an express train two miles from **Lourdes**.
■ The Toledo Alcazar falls to government troops with relief columns only five miles away.
. . . ABYSSINIA is allowed a seat in the Assembly of the League of Nations by 39-4 votes, with 6 abstentions

---

HOW SOME OF THE TOP SHARES HAVE BEEN PERFORMING ON THE LONDON STOCK EXCHANGE

BRITISH STOCKS		INDUSTRIALS			
War 3½ p.c.	106¼	Anglo-Newf'dl'ds	34/41½	Met. Elec. Sup.	54/-
Conv. 3 p.c.	105⅝	Ditto Opts.	15·6	Raleigh	51/9
Conv. 3½ p.c.	107⅞	Ditto 4½ p.c. Deb.	106	Ranks (5/-)	17/6
Conv. 4½ p.c.	117 7-16	Assoc. Equip.	44/-	Reed, A. E. Ord.	39/-
Conv. 5 p.c.	120¾	Ass. News. Dfd.	25/9	Reed, A. E., Pref.	28/6
Conv. 2½ p.c.	102	Ditto Notes	106½	Rolls-Royce	8 5-16
Cons. 4 p.c.	114½	Ass. Ptld. Cement	70/3	South Durham	49/9xd
Cons. 2½ p.c.	85⅝	Austin	46/9	Spillers Ord	65/-
Fund. 4 p.c.	117⅞	Babcock, Wilcox	54/3	Stew. & L. Dfd.	36/10½
Fund. 3 p.c.	103½	J. Barker	80/9	Sudan Plants.	35/-
Fund. 2½ p.c.	18d1s	Bass	134/6	Sunday Pict. Ord.	48/-
Locals 3 p.c.	96⅝	Bats	6 3-32	Sunday Pict. Pref.	32/-
Victory Bonds	116½	Bleachers	7/-	Tate & Lyle	89/9
HOME RAILS		Cable & W. Pfd.	108	Tob. S. Tst. Ord.	4 7-16
Gt. Western	50⅝	Cable & W. "A"	29¾	Ditto Dfd.	4 13-16
L.M.S. Ord.	19⅝	Carreras "A"	9 1-16	Turner & Newall	75/3
L.M.S. 4 p.c. 1st Pf.	84½	Cerebos	11 11-16	Unilever	33/-
L.M.S. '23 Pf.	58	Coats	66/-	U. Steel	32/-
L.N.E. Dfd.	5½	Co. of Ldn. Elec.	58/41½	Vickers	22/3
L.N.E. 5 p.c. Pfd.	9¾	Cory, Wm.	82/9	Watney Defd.	79/6
L.N.E. 4 p.c. 1st Pf.	58	Courtaulds	59/9	Woolworths	118.6xd
L.N.E. 4 p.c. 2nd Pf.	20¼	D.M. & G Trust	55/9		
Southern Dfd	23	D. Mirror Ord.	23/41½	**OILS**	
Southern Pfd.	87	D. Mirror Debs.	106	Anglo-Iranian	79/41½
Transport "C"	109½	D. Mirror Pref.	33/-	Burmah Oil	91/3
FOREIGN RAILS		Dennis	31/41½	Dutch	32⅛
B.A. Gt. Sth.	23	Distillers	99/6xd	Eagles. Mex.	9/41½
B.A. Western	18½	Dorman, Long	20/9	Eagles Can.	8/1½
B.A. Pacific	10½	Dunlops	42/-	Phœnix (1/-)	5/-
Cent. Argentine	14	Eno Props.	11/3	Shells	90/-
BANKS		Ford	35/3	Trin. Leases	95/-
Barclays "B"	78·6	Gen. Electric	81/3	V.O.C.	42/6
Lloyds "A"	62/7½	Guest, Keen	34/6		
Midland £1	94/-xd	Guinness	158/-	**MINES**	
Nat. Prov. £4	155⅝xd	Harrods	84/-	Ashanti	59/3xd
West. £4, £1 pd	96·6xd	Hawkers	28·9	Burma Corps.	10/41½
ANGLO-AMERICANS		Henley's Teleg'ph	7 7-32	Chartered	23/10½xd
Braz. Tracs.	$105⅝	Imp. Airways	53/9	Crowns	14
Can. Pacs.	$11 9-16	Imp. Chem. Ord	37/6	Daggafontein	8¼
E.M.I.	27·6	Imps.	155/7½	De Beers Dfd.	7 3-16
Hydro-Electric	$6	I. Tea Stores	37/3	East Geduld	9 15-16
Int. Nickel	$48½	Johnson & Phillips	50/-	East Rand	62/5
Radio	$14 5-16	Marks & Sp.	5/- . . 96·3	Geduld	10⅞
U.S. Steel	$49⅛			Gen. Mining	97/6
				G. Coast Sel.	25/-
				Gold Fields	76/10½

HELLO... AND GOODBYE...

HELLO ...

Edward VIII and George VI, *right*

Oakland Bay Bridge, San Francisco

Spitfire Mark 1

Wellington Bomber

Television for everyone

Gatwick Airport

Transatlantic flying: Pan-Am

St Neots Quads

Queen Mary, *bottom*

Dame Laura Knight–the first woman RA

Air records by the dozen

The Davis Cup (for the 4th year in succession!)

Pets Corner at London Zoo

Spanish Civil War, *right*.

Fascist Riots in London, *below, right*.

The Black Box

Boxer dogs, *far right*

Leslie Mitchell–first male TV announcer

Bare legs at Ascot

Budget leaks

TIM–the Talking Clock

Jarrow marchers *(far right)*

Heatwave in Alaska

False fingernails
The first Hit Parade, in *Billboard* magazine

GOODBYE

George V

Edward VIII

G K Chesterton

M R James

Federico Garcia Lorca

Louis Bleriot

Freedom of speech in Germany

Horses in Regent Street and New Bond Street

John Gilbert

Maxim Gorky

The Crystal Palace, *far left*

Sir Edward German, composer

Louis Bleriot

Frank Hornby

B J T Bosanquet (inventor of the googly)

Sir Edgar Britten, captain of the Queen Mary

Dame Clara Butt

Dr Ivan Pavlov

Rudyard Kipling

A E Houseman

24 Thursday

Princess Juliana of the Netherlands is to marry at the end of January or early February next year. The honeymoon will be spent in southern Europe.

■ **Mussolini** is expected to withdraw Italian representatives from the League of Nations in protest against the 'insult' of the admission of the Abyssinian delegation.

. . . Sarah Churchill and comedian Vic Oliver are officially engaged . . .

25 Friday

Dockers, zoo keepers and sailors take part in a **badger hunt** on board a Russian motorship in the Thames. The badger is part of an exchange consignment of birds, animals and reptiles from Moscow. He and his mate escape and go to ground behind the cargo in the hold. The female is quickly captured, but they cannot get hold of the male until all the cargo is unloaded. Pick of the exchange are four Bactrian camels and a Siberian tiger.

26 Saturday

The Ritz Hotel in Barcelona, formerly one of the most luxurious in that city, has been taken over by the Catalan government and is used as Hotel Gastronomic No 1 for the Socialist Union General de Trabajadores and the Syndicalist Confederacion Nacional de Trabajo.

■ England's biggest municipal **power station** is opened at Fulham. It cost £3,820,000.

■ The LNER *Silver Jubilee*, Britain's first stream-lined passenger train, knocks 36min of the usual journey time between Newcastle and Edinburgh.

27 Sunday

In Buffalo, New York, Ernest Biegazski unveils a barrel called Nuda, in which he hopes to sail across the Atlantic. It is an iron bound oak barrel with bundles of cork on the sides to keep it on an even keel, and it has a sail, a rudder and a keel.

■ Mrs Bruno Hauptmann, widow of the Lindbergh baby **kidnapper** who was later executed for his murder, says she is on the verge of a discovery that will clear her husband's name.

■ Insurgent troops under General Varela take Toledo from the Government militia just in time to rescue the defenders of the Alcazar making their **last stand** in the ruins. 1,500 people were found alive, including 400 women and children.

28 Monday

Millions of sprats stray into Bridport Harbour, Dorset. The fishermen's wives help land the fish. The biggest catch is 190 bushels, or about two million sprats, weighing nearly two tons.

■ Sq Ldr F R D Swain captures the world **altitude record** reaching a height of 49,967 feet (over nine miles) in a specially adapted Bristol 138 Monoplane. He wears a special pressurized suit and breathing gear.

29 Tuesday

The start of the Rand Air Race from Portsmouth, England to Johannesburg, South Africa, a distance of 6,150 miles. There are nine competing machines, four solo and five with two pilots. First prize for the pilot making the fastest time is £4,000.

HIT SONGS OF 1936

At The Balalaika
Hawaiian War Chant
Hear My Song
I'll Walk Beside You
Is it True What They Say About Dixie?
It's Delovely
I've Got You Under My Skin
Let's Face The Music and Dance
Mexicali Rose
Pennies From Heaven
Small Hotel
These Foolish Things
The Way You Look Tonight

30 Wednesday
Full Moon

The Postmaster General inaugurates the first post office on wheels. It takes all post office facilities to race meetings, agricultural shows and other open-air events and includes telephone kiosks, telegraph, automatic stamp machines and a post box. It has an awning to protect customers from the rain, and a duck-board for use in a field.

JARROW MEN'S MARCH FOR JOBS

OCT
5

THE JARROW CRUSADE marchers leave on their long march to London, above. The men, many of whom have been out of work for years, hope that by drawing attention to their plight something might be done to bring their town back to life. The Unemployment Assistance Board refuses to pay the men's dependents relief for the first three days of the march. A medical student marches with them to look after their health, and they are joined by a stray black dog they name Paddy. All along the way they are met by people offering encouragement, support, accommodation and food. At Loughborough, Labour MP for Jarrow, Ellen Wilkinson, says she will march the rest of the way with them. They arrive in London on November 1, right, but no member of the government will meet them. They return home by special train. 200 fog detonators explode in welcome at the station.

OCTOBER

1 Thursday

After 25 years' residence in Buckingham Palace, Queen Mary moves to her new home at Marlborough House.

■ The BBC sends out a request to the **Herring Fleet** that the number of nets to be shot should be limited to eight per man, and boats out of Yarmouth and Lowestoft must return by Saturday, to avoid a glut.

■ At Burgos, **General Franco** is proclaimed dictator and head of the National Government of all Spain held by the rebels.

2 Friday

Portsmouth-Johannesburg Race — only one plane finishes, piloted by C W A Scott and Giles Guthrie. They cover the 6,154 miles in 52hrs 56mins 48.2secs at an average speed of 123mph.

■ Mayors of all East London boroughs ask the Home Office to ban the planned Fascist march through their districts on Sunday.

■ Bournmouth Corporation bans Noel Coward's play, *Fumed Oak*, and D H Lawrence's *My Son, My Son*. A Bristol woman who has seen both plays says, 'I have never seen anything more **disgusting.**

I was ashamed to be in the theatre.'

■ Preparations are being made to evacuate British women and children from the **Yangtse** ports following reports that the Chinese are evacuating Hongchew and the Jap-controlled areas of Shanghai and Chapei.

3 Saturday

Jean Batten (26), the New Zealand flyer, arrives at Lympne, Kent to start her 12,000 mile **solo flight** to New Zealand at 4 am, in the same plane in which she flew the South Atlantic. She will make her first stop at Marseilles for petrol.

■ **Pam Barton** (19) from Guildford, Surrey, wins the US Women's Golf Championship in New Jersey, and now holds both the British and American titles.

■ Mrs Miles, the mother of the St Neots quads, turns down the offer of £10,000 for Ann, from a lady who had travelled from Scotland just to see the quads but refused to give her name.

4 Sunday

64 people are arrested and 268 injured as hundreds stampede in London riots. The Fascists meet a counter demonstration when **Sir Oswald Mosley**, *below,* is told his meeting and parade cannot take place.

■ 2,300 arrested at Parc des Prince, Paris. The National Party stage a protest parade outside a stadium where 30,000 Communists are meeting.

5 Monday

The **Jarrow marchers**, set off for London on their March for Jobs. *(See page 77).* They will sleep tonight at Chester-le-Street in halls and schools, provided by the local council.

■ The Dupath Well, or the Well of the Beautiful Lady at Callington, Cornwall, which dates back more than 1,200 years, has been acquired by the Cornwall Society on behalf of the nation. The water in the well is always icy cold, and legend has it that it was the site of a duel when both combatants were killed. The lady erected a stone baptistry over the well.

. . . New Zealand flyer JEAN BATTEN arrives at Brindisi, Italy and leaves for Cyprus.

6 Tuesday

Jean Batten arrives at the Iraq Petroleum Company's pumping station between Baghdad and Damascus.

■ Cunard signs the contract with John Brown & Co for a

SLEEK, STREAMLINED GIANTS OF THE TRACKS

Three of the proud, streamlined giants of the LNMR which haul the Silver Jubilee expresses between London and Newcastle. Cleaners at work on (from left) Quicksilver, Silver Link and Silver Fox.

sister ship to the *Queen Mary*.

■ Two 14-year-olds try to join the **Jarrow Marchers** at Ferryhill, Co Durham. The marchers set off again after breakfast of tea, bread and jam. The miners present the marchers with 120lbs of slab cake.

7 Wednesday

Princess Assah of Iraq, who married an Italian waiter earlier this year, turns down an offer of £30,000 for them to play royal lovers in a film.

■ George Andrew McMahon, who attempted to **assassinate** the King, issues writs against 263 cinemas showing the incident on Constitution Hill on July 16.

■ Four Jarrow marchers are on the **sick** list, and Paddy, the black dog who has become their mascot, is treated for inflamed feet.

8 Thursday

New Zealand flyer Jean Batten arrives in Akyab, Burma. She has reached here one day earlier than any previous flight.

■ **Lord Nuffield** gives £1 million to Oxford University for a post-graduate medical school.

9 Friday

The Bishop of Ripon greets the **Jarrow Marchers**. He will hold a special service for them on Sunday afternoon

■ Three famous architects, Sir Giles Gilbert Scott, Sir James Grey West, and Mr G Grey Wernum, are planning the **Coronation** decorations, to ensure they are an artistic triumph.

10 Saturday

Halifax Fire Brigade save the life of a sparrow which falls down a street drain. They retrieve it from the drain and administer oxygen.

■ **Gaumont** British Film Corporation will remain under British control when Associated British Pictures take control after a three

MOSELEY'S BLACK SHIRTS SPARK

SIR OSWALD MOSELEY, 6th Baronet, founded the British Union of Fascists in 1932, supported by newspaper proprietor Viscount Rothermere. Early October sees trouble in the East End of London. Jewish shopkeepers ask the police to intervene and the Fascists clash with counter demonstrators when Sir Oswald is told that his meeting and parade cannot take place. Top left: Sir Oswald Moseley; Above and left: Anti-Fascist demonstrators are led away under arrest. Bottom right: Police tear down barricades in Cable Street. Far right: Police charge crowds near Aldgate where hundreds gather to protest against the Fascist march on October 5.

EAST END RIOTING

months' struggle to keep it out of American hands. The new chain will have 650 cinemas.

11 Sunday

Uproar in London's **East End** when Communists and Fascists clash.(*See panel*).

■ **Jean Batten** reaches Darwin, Australia having smashed H F Broadbent's record solo flight of England-Australia in 6days 21hrs 19mins by 26hrs 16mins. The Australian Federal Aviation authorities are talking of banning her flight across the Tasman Sea as they are opposed to single-engine planes attempting this trip.

12 Monday

Australian Federal Aviation authorities say Jean Batten can continue her flight.

■ A ship carrying an entire tube station and a garage for 25 cars makes her maiden Channel crossing. *The Hampton Ferry* enables her passengers to board at Victoria at 10pm and not be disturbed until a customs officer calls them 30min outside Paris, where they will arrive at 8.55am

■ The Zeppelin **Hindenburg**, en route to Frankfurt on its last trip this year, is given special permission to pass over Leeds, Bradford and Grimsby because of adverse weather conditions.

. . . The death is announced of the famous cricketer B J T Bosanquet, who evolved the 'googly'. He would have been 59 today . . .

13 Tuesday

Opening of the film of *Romeo and Juliet* starring Leslie Howard and Norma Shearer, with Basil Rathbone as Tybalt and John Barrymore as Mercutio.

. . . The first SNOW of winter falls on Ben Nevis . . .

■ Following a Cabinet meeting, No 10 issues a statement that Ministers have no intention of meeting the **Jarrow marchers**.

14 Wednesday

4,500 miles of trunk roads are to have more anti-glare hedges and pedestrian guard rails.

■ 4,000 policemen line the approaches to the

East End when 5,000 of Sir Oswald Mosley's **Fascists march** in. Sir Oswald makes a speech from a loudspeaker van.
. . . Rain all over the UK ends the official drought— 14 days without rain . . .

15 Thursday

30th International **Motor Show** opens at Olympia. Nearly 500 cars are on show, ranging in price from £100-£3,000, from the UK, Germany, France, the USA, Italy and Canada, together with caravans, trailers, motor boats, garages and gadgets.
■ With a rubber boat on board but no radio, airwoman **Jean Batten** sets out across the Tasman Sea.
■ Lord Nuffield gives £80,000 to Guy's Hospital for an extension to the Nurses' Home.
. . . A Roman Catholic priest at Princes Risborough, Bucks, who prayed to St Theresa every day for £3,000 to build a church, is given the money on condition he never reveals the name of his benefactor . . .

16 Friday

Only half as much soot is deposited on Glasgow than 20 years ago (250 tons per square mile).
■ After a perilous, storm-battered, journey **Jean Batten** lands in Auckland and is met by a tumultuous crowd. She has flown from England to New Zealand in 11days 1hr 25min, and crossed from Sydney in the record time of 9hr 29min.
■ 19 new islands have been discovered by the Soviet ice breaker *Sedov* in the vicinity of the Nordenscheld Archipelago of the Arctic.

17 Saturday

Two passenger planes flying between Glasgow and Skye summon help to a ship on the rocks at Islay. The pilot of one plane tells the other, who veers off course to establish the position of the steamer. He calls the control tower at Renfrew, who tell Lloyds, who send out the Islay life boat. Tugs go out from Glasgow to refloat the ship.

18 Sunday

An earthquake just before dawn in the Venice area kills 15.
■ *The New York American* says as a breed Englishwomen 'seem to run to narrow shoulders, flat chests, lanky legs and big feet,' but 'when it comes to charm, ease of manner, animation and a lack of strain and overtiredness, they are several steps in the lead' of American women.

19 Monday

More quakes shake Venice. The death toll is now 34. There is no major damage to the city.
■ Imperial Airways and Pan American Airways will start experimental flights between Ireland and the USA next March.
■ Mrs Grace Bagnato, one of the favoured contestants in the Toronto Baby Marathon, is fighting for her life and the life of her baby. Mrs B already has **23 children**, nine of

whom were born during the period of the contest and expects the tenth to be born before October 31 when it ends. Mrs B is suffering from a debilitated condition and has already had one blood transfusion.

20 Tuesday

On her way back from Paris, **Amy Mollison** loses her way in fog and crash lands in a field at Chelsfield, Kent. She says she and her husband are to separate and she will fly under her maiden name Amy Johnson.

■ The **Earl of Warwick**, who has gone to Hollywood to make a fortune in the movies, has been given his Hollywood screen name. He will be known as Michael Brooke.

21 Wednesday

Court Mourning ends today.

■ The British Embassy in Madrid will remain open whatever happens.

. . . Jim Mollison in New York expresses surprise at his wife Amy's statement that they are to separate . . .

22 Thursday

Mrs Anne Smith is a surprise entry in the Toronto Baby Marathon. She has registered nine children, but the other mothers think she might be keeping a couple in reserve.

■ The MCC team in Australia is struck by **injuries.** R W V Robbins, fractured finger; Duckworth, finger injury; Leyland and Ames, back trouble, and now Fagg has an injured thumb. They are without a wicket keeper as Fagg was deputising for Ames.

■ The **infant mortality** rate in the UK is the lowest on record at 57 per 1,000 births.

23 Friday

A yacht, a motor car and a magnificent carpet made by the women of Rotterdam will be among the presents for Princess Juliana and Prince Bernhard when they marry.

■ The **favourite drink** in Hungary is a cocktail invented by the King when he was Prince of Wales: apricot brandy and bitters, rye whisky, water, a lump of sugar and some orange peel.

■ Littlehampton will celebrate the Coronation with four homes for needy families with four bedrooms, electric light and low rent.

■ 3,000 Scottish fisher girls close the ports of Gt Yarmouth, Lowestoft and Gorleston, and bring the East Anglian herring industry to a standstill. They are demanding a further 2d. a barrel for their work.

24 Saturday

Rheumatism costs Britain £17 million a year—more cases than the combined total of diabetes, heart disease, TB and cancer.

■ The world's **fattest baby** title will shortly be claimed for Joseph Randazza of Boston, USA, who will be four on Christmas Eve. He already weighs 10st 6lbs. The current holder is Leslie Bowles of Yarmouth (4) who weighs 11st.

25 Sunday

Torrential rain and hail with gale-force winds sweep Britian. Five lifeboats are launched.

■ Mr Ernie Clark is to fly from Lympne for New Zealand at dawn. He will follow Jean Batten's route and hopes to beat her time.

26 Monday

The *Queen Mary* arrives at Southampton with more than 50 injured passengers and crew after two days of storms. Twice the ship had to slow to 14 knots so the surgeon could perform emergency operations.

■ Britain is amazed by reports from New York that the **King** is to wed in June.

27 Tuesday

Mrs Wallis Simpson, *left*, is granted a decree nisi at Ipswich Assizes from Mr Ernest Aldrich Simpson. Mrs Simpson's case was that the marriage was happy until 1934 when her husband began to stay out often at night. Misconduct was alleged between Mr Simpson and a woman at the Hotel de

Paris at Bray. The hearing lasts 23min.

■George Andrew McMahon's leave to appeal is dismissed (see September 14).

■ British film star **Merle Oberon** is to marry **David Niven**. She is returning home to play opposite Charles Laughton in the film of *I, Claudius*.

■ **Gales** sweep Britain. 11 places in Scotland cut off. 15 are drowned when the lightship capsizes at Cuxhaven.

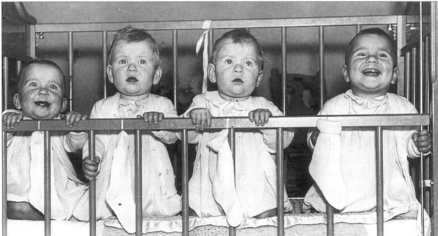

28 Wednesday

Westminster Abbey is to have an extra 3,000 seats for the Coronation at a cost of £30,000. The Abbey will be closed in June and handed over to the Duke of Norfolk who, as Earl Marshal, will organise the extension.

■ Sir Edgar Britten, captain of the *Queen Mary* dies. He was found unconscious on the floor of his cabin and died six hours later in a Southampton nursing home.

29 Thursday

Jim Mollison leaves Harbour Grace, Newfoundland at 8.40pm GMT. He hopes to reach Croydon in 14-16hr. He has with him soup, six apples, barley sugar, the watch he lent Beryl Markham, a good luck cable from Amy and no radio.

■ **Lord Nuffield** is to help modernise the mechanized side of the Army and RAF ground services, and his Wolverhampton aero factory will produce tank engines.

30 Friday

A doctor in Alberta, Canada, is treating a 24yr-old gold-mining engineer with pneumonia, by telephone. The camp, 800 miles away, is cut off as the ice is not thick enough for a plane to land and the snow is too soft for a dog team. The only medicines available at the gold camp are iodine and whisky. The doctor says let him inhale the iodine, and give him $\frac{1}{2}$fl oz of whisky every three hours.

■ The King suggests that **Coronation Day** should be a school holiday.

. . . Jim Mollison crosses from Harbour Grace, Newfoundland to Croydon in 13hr 17min, at an average speed of 200mph and an altitude of 15,000ft.

31 Saturday

The **St Neots Quads**, *above*, may become Britain's youngest tax payers. They have had 20,000 visitors since their new nursery was opened in July, and now an official wants to charge them entertainment tax. Their mother Mrs Miles says the money goes to pay off the cost of the nursery and its maintenance, but the tax man wants 2d. of every shilling paid.

■ The **Nobel Prize** for Medicine is awarded to Sir Henry Hallett Dale of the National Institute for Medical Research, London and Professor Otto Loewi of Graz, Austria for their work on the chemical transmission of nervous effects.

NOVEMBER

1 Sunday

Mussolini offers England and France a peace pact. He will will not interfere with their Mediterranean routes, but demands that

Italy's 'vital rights and interests' are respected, meaning that he would like Britain to recognize Italian Abyssinia.

■ More than 2½ million people in the USA are learning to tap dance. Teachers say it is all down to Fred, Ginger and Shirley Temple.

2 Monday

State Opening of Parliament. Torrential rain causes the King to cancel the State drive. Florence Horsburgh, MP for Dundee, becomes the first woman to move the Address.

■ 40 tons of liquid concrete flooring crashes through the centre of the new £1 million **Earls Court** Exhibition building. Incredibly, no-one is killed though 12 are injured.

■ In Australia, **Wally Hammond**, *right*, scores a century against South Australia in Adelaide, becoming the first Englishman to score four successive hundreds in Australia. MCC are all out for 236 in the 2nd innings.

3 Tuesday

Sir John Jarvis, Jarrow's fairy godfather, has plans for new industries in the town financed by himself, one of the big banks and the Special Areas Reconstruction Association. He does not expect to make a profit.

■ **President Roosevelt** is re-elected with the most sweeping victory in US history. He takes 23,160,365 votes against Landon's 14,423,777.

4 Wednesday

If you want to rent a service flat in St James's for the week of the Coronation next year, it will cost you £472.

■ The Lord Mayor of London announces that a statue of **George V** will be erected on a site facing the Houses of Parliament and Westminster Abbey.

■ Queen Mary and the Princess Royal pack gift baskets for hospital patients at the Imperial Institute. For 20 years the Queen has supervised the dispatch of clothes sent to her for the Queen Mary Needlework Guild.

5 Thursday

The London Fire Brigade answers 164 **Guy Fawkes** calls.

■ Ernie Clarke, who left Lympne 10 days ago, lands in Darwin. He is being held in quarantine because he has not been vaccinated.

■ The **Jarrow marchers return** with Paddy, the dog who became their mascot. He has a new collar and licence in the name of the Crusaders, paid from the marchers' fund.

6 Friday

Shells rain down on **Madrid.** 200 British subjects shelter in the embassy. A vast Union Jack has been painted on the roof, and flags surround the perimeter.

■ From January 1 next year, BBC's *Children's Hour* will run for an hour instead of the present 45mins.

7 Saturday

Four masked men burst into the 200ft Wallace Monument above Stirling and steal one of Scotland's most famous relics — the sword of Sir William Wallace.

■ **Spanish Government flees** to Valencia leaving General Miaja to defend Madrid.

8 Sunday

Madrid in flames. Doctors cannot estimate the numbers of dead and wounded.

■ **Remembrance Day**. 10,000 services held across the country.

■ Poland's Foreign Minister, Colonel Beck, arrives for talks in London with his own police guard, an inspector, a sergeant and two privates, all in plain clothes. Mrs Beck is said to be the most beautiful woman in Poland.

9 Monday

11,000 people see John Henry Lewis (USA) beat Len Harvey (GB) for the World Light Heavyweight title at Wembley, on points.
■ The Lord Mayor's Show is the shortest on record and lasts just 3¼hrs.
■ Tennis champion **Fred Perry** signs a contract to turn professional. He is expected to make £20,000 a year.
■ Mrs Elizabeth Frisby is elected High Sheriff of Leicestershire — the first woman to hold the post in its 650 year history.

10 Tuesday

The government of Ontario is considering dividing the prize money in the Toronto Baby Marathon between all the children of the contestants born within the period.
■ The German ambassador, von Ribbentrop, receives Lord Burghley, Lord Portal, Capt Evan Hunter, Sir Noel Curtis-Bennett and Dr A E Porritt and presents them with the Ensign of the 1st Class of the German Olympic Order on behalf of the Führer and Chancellor.

11 Wednesday

The King lays a wreath at the Cenotaph in Whitehall.
■ 70mph **gales** sweep Britain and force the destroyers and submarines anchored in Portland Harbour for the King's visit to the fleet tomorrow out of their anchorage and round to Weymouth Bay.
■ Death of the composer Sir Edward German (74), probably best known for his light opera *Merrie England*. Born at Whitchurch, Salop, he learned to play the organ aged five.

12 Thursday

American writer Eugene O'Neill is awarded the **Nobel Prize** for literature.
■ The new **Bay Bridge**, *right*, is opened by the Governor of California.

8½ miles long, it links San Francisco with Oakland.

13 Friday

For the third time this year Chrysler and Dodge workers get a bonus. This year Chrysler have given their workers £1,660,000.
. . . The funeral of composer Sir Edward German. By his express wish, no music is played . . .

14 Saturday

Queen Mary pays an informal visit to the East End. She calls at the new Peoples' Palace in Mile End Road, and Queen Mary's College.

15 Sunday

The London to Brighton Old Crocks Race commemorates Emancipation Day, the run of 1896 when the 'Red Flag' Act was abolished. The 1903 Wolseley that won the fourth group (1903-4) was found on a rubbish dump in Devon, but is in its original condition.
■ **Ernie Clark**, released from quarantine in Darwin, lands at Blenheim, NZ, after flying from England in 30 days.
■ World Champion **roller skater** Bill Weatherall, is stopped on doctor's orders from beating his own non-stop record of 128hr 48min at the skating rink at Methil,

Fife. He is taken off the floor at midnight having skated 124½ hr non stop.

16 Monday

An LMS train, *Princess Elizabeth,* covers the 401½ miles between Euston and Glasgow in a world record time of 5hr 53min at an average speed of 68.2mph. At Tring the train is doing 95mph.

■ Spanish rebels gain a foothold in University City, two miles from Puerta del Sol, the Piccadilly of Madrid.

■ **Mary Pickford** (43), 'The World's Sweetheart', is to marry **Charles (Buddy) Rogers** (32) film star and dance band leader.

17 Tuesday

Marconi, ridden by D Morgan, the first horse to race in the King's colours, comes in 10th.

■ Prince Bernhard zur Lippe Biesterfeld is received in a farewell audience by Hitler. He will become a Dutch citizen on his marriage to Princess Juliana of the Netherlands.

■ British film star **Valerie Hobson** (19), is signed by **Douglas Fairbanks Jr** to play opposite him in *Forever and Ever*.

■ The driver of the LMS train *Princess Elizabeth*, sets another new record on the way back to Euston from Glasgow of 5hrs 44mins at an average speed of 70mph.

18 Wednesday

King Edward VIII, *right*, visits distressed areas in South Wales. At Dowlais, once a flourishing steel works but idle for six years, he walks through a scene of desolation and is visibly distressed. 'These works brought these people here,' he said. 'Something ought to be done to find them employment.'

... Italy and Germany recognise the Spanish REBEL government ...

19 Thursday

Thousands of acorns, harvested in Windsor Great Park, have been sent to the Dominions and Crown Colonies for a chain of commemorative oak trees to be planted to celebrate the coronation.

■ Father Ronald Knox, chaplain to Roman Catholic undergraduates at Oxford and writer of detective stories, is appointed domestic prelate to the **Pope**.

20 Friday

Rather than dump 10,000 herring back into the sea, Exmouth fishermen offer them to the Mayor of Exeter for distribution to the poor.

■ Britain has a system of **air raid warnings** that will alert the country within 7-10mins of raiders crossing the coast.

■ A Bill now before Parliament allows 'every person who has been in the same employment for 12 months or longer to eight clear consecutive days holiday with pay once a year'.

21 Saturday

Because of the severity of the winter weather conditions, no further attemps will be made on the world altitude record by RAF pilots until the spring.

■ **Gold bullion** worth £3 million arrives from France by Channel steamer. It is thought to be part of a large quantity removed from Spain by the Madrid government.

22 Sunday

Fog blankets the UK from London to Perth.
■ Lord Burghley, who, it is rumoured, may become Minister of Physical Education in Britain is in Stockholm to spend three days studying Swedish drill methods.
■ Only four film stars have perfect voices for the movies, says John Livadary, who is in charge of recording for one of the main film studios — Bing Crosby, William Powell, Clive Brook and Jean Arthur.

23 Monday

The engagement is announced of the **Duke of Norfolk** (28) to the Hon Lavinia Strutt (20), daughter of Lord Belper.
■ Fog is so thick at Warwick races that a policeman is stationed in the centre of the course, about a furlong from the winning post. He has to whistle the winners home.
. . . An AVALANCHE in Alaska cuts the city of Juneau in half. 20 people feared dead . . .

24 Tuesday

All British naval leave in Malta is stopped and the flagship of the Mediterranean fleet, *HMS Cyclops,* leaves for Spanish waters accompanied by eight submarines.
■ **Lord Nuffield** increases his £1,250,000 gift to Oxford University for medical research by a further £750,000, 'so that the scheme shall be complete'.

25 Wednesday

The Medical Research Council is to investigate the use of **yellow headlights**, following French proposals for their use.
■ Convicts in prisons are making gas masks, military sandbags, small aeroplane parts and ambulance boxes (5,000 gas masks alone are made in Maidstone Gaol every week).

26 Thursday

Although Army recruitment is well below required levels, the government says no to

conscription.
■ US newspapers report that former US society woman **Mrs Wallis Simpson** has had her life threatened, and that special guards have been engaged to protect her.
■ Germany protests at the award of the Nobel Peace Prize to Carl von Ossietsky, the German pacifist writer.

27 Friday

US newspapers say there is no truth in their story about death threats to Mrs Simpson.
■ The St Neots **Quads** are one today. 130 telegrams pour in from all over the world.
. . . Dr Goebbels bans criticism of art, literature and other works in Germany . . .

DESTROYED!

NOV 30

It takes just 20 minutes for a famous London landmark to be tragically engulfed by fire. Flames 300ft high light up the sky and can be seen from aeroplanes in mid-Channel and the Devil's Dyke, nr Brighton. 90 fire engines and 500 firemen from every station in London fight the blaze. 3,000 policemen cordon off the area. The Duke of Kent arrives at 11.30pm and is still there at 3am.

28 Saturday

A new fire engine is causing embarrassment to Jerusalem councillors. They forgot when they ordered it that there are no high-pressure water hydrants in Jerusalem.

■ **Gordon Richards** achieves '1,000 rides in a season' in the last race of the Flat racing season. His record is: Won 177, 2nd 160, 3rd 108, unplaced 555. He is the first jockey to have ridden 1,000 races in one season and he wins his tenth jockey's championship.

29 Sunday

Jim Mollison and his co-pilot Edouard Cornighon-Molinier take off from Croydon at 9.30am in an attempt to win the England-

Cape Town record by getting to the Cape and back in five days.

■ Foot-and-mouth disease in the Midlands. No movement of cattle is permitted within 15 miles of infected premises.

■ *The Daily Telegraph* appeal for a new organ for Westminster Abbey for the Coronation reaches £12,262 10s.

30 Monday

Lord Nuffield announces a profit-sharing fund for his workforce, transferring one million stock units to a trust fund.

■ **Crystal Palace**, London'2 £1½ million showpiece entertainment centre on Sydenham Hill, is completely destroyed by **fire** *(see panel, above)*.

DECEMBER

1 Tuesday

Between 5,000-6,000 German troops land in Spain and go to Seville, the Nationalist HQ.
■ Jim Mollison and his co-pilot are long overdue. They leave Kimberley to fly less than 500 miles to Cape Town, are seen flying along the coast by a lighthouse keeper at Cape Agulhas, 100 miles southeast of Cape Town at 3.30pm, but have not been spotted since.

2 Wednesday

First hint of **Constitutional crisis:** Prime Minister Mr Baldwin has an audience with the King. The Cabinet 'has been compelled to face a situation of extreme delicacy and difficulty in connection with the king's future domestic life which, unless satisfactorily solved, must lead to a constitutional crisis of the gravest possible character.'
■ **Leon Trotsky**, *left*, staying in Norway, must find a new place of refuge. His permit expires in December.

3 Thursday

Intense world interest in the monarchy issue. Headlines 3-ins high in the *New York Times*: KING AND COUNTRY DEADLOCKED OVER MRS SIMPSON. EDWARD MAY ABDICATE IN FAVOUR OF YORK.
Britain is astounded by the news. The Royal family cancel all engagements. *(See p92-3)*
■ Jim Mollison and his co-pilot are found on a farm 100 miles SE of Cape Town. They were forced to land when they ran out of petrol.
■ The writer Thomas

Mann (author of *Buddenbrooks, Death in Venice*, etc) is one of 39 to be deprived of German citizenship.

4 Friday

The King, his ministers and representatives of the Dominions are still engaged in discussions over the King's desire to marry **Mrs Simpson**. The Dominion governments make it quite clear that neither as queen nor as a 'morganatic wife' would Mrs Simpson be accepted by the peoples of the Dominions. Mr Baldwin makes a statement in the House of Commons saying the government would not introduce legislation whereby the King could marry Mrs Simpson but she would not become queen. Mrs Simpson leaves Britain by chauffeur-driven car, and is believed to be making for Cannes on the French Riviera.
■ **First Test** in Brisbane, Australia. England win the toss and elect to bat.
■ The keel of No 552, the sister ship to the *Queen Mary*, is laid at the John Brown shipyard in Clydebank.

5 Saturday

Manufacturers of Coronation souvenir goods stop production awaiting the outcome of the Constitutional crisis. Mr Baldwin spends an hour with the King at his home at Fort Belvedere, near Windsor. The Archbishop of Canterbury spends 50 mins with Mr Baldwin. who later has a meeting with Queen Mary. Mrs Simpson arrives in Cannes and goes to stay with friends.
■ CRICKET: In the First Test in Australia, the MCC score 339-8 in their 1st innings.

6 Sunday

CRISIS: The crowds outside 10 Downing Street are so great the street is cleared. Newsreel cameramen surround the villa in Cannes where Mrs Simpson is staying.
■ Snow in London — the first this month.
. . . The Mexican government will

PAGE FOR EVERY HOUSEWIFE PAGE 27
THURSDAY
Dec. 3rd, 1936

Daily Mirror

THE DAILY PICTURE NEWSPAPER WITH THE LARGEST NET SALE   ONE PENNY

QUIET CORNER - Page 16 | CASSANDRA - - - 14 | STARS' MESSAGE - 21 | AMUSEMENTS - - 20 | BROADCASTING - - 3
BELINDA - - - - 26 | RUGGLES - - - 29 | SERIAL AND FIFE - 22 | DOROTHY DIX - - 26 | PIP & SQUEAK - - 5

THE KING WANTS TO MARRY MRS. SIMPSON: CABINET ADVISES 'NO'

THE KING, THE "DAILY MIRROR" UNDERSTANDS, HAS TOLD THE CABINET OF HIS WISH TO MARRY MRS. SIMPSON, AMERICAN-BORN SOCIETY WOMAN NOW LIVING IN LONDON. THE CABINET HAS ADVISED AGAINST IT.

LAST NIGHT THE KING AND THE PRIME MINISTER DISCUSSED THE MATTER AT BUCKINGHAM PALACE.

grant asylum to **LEON TROTSKY** as soon as he makes a formal request.

7 Monday

In the First Test, **Australia** lose 5 wickets for 202 runs.
■ **CRISIS:** In a statement to the House of Commons, Mr Baldwin says the King has not yet made up his mind what to do. In Cannes, Mrs Simpson says she wishes to avoid 'anything that would hurt or damage His Majesty or the Throne, and should such action solve the problem would be willing to withdraw from a situation that has been rendered both unhappy and untenable.' Radio stations in the USA open at 6am local time to hear the live broadcasts from London.

8 Tuesday

Preparations for raising the Coronation stands in the Mall continue. Mr Baldwin, summoned to Fort Belvedere, spends five hours with the King and his brothers, York and Kent.
■ Eric Shipton, the Everest mountaineer who has just returned from surveying the Himalayas, saw footprints resembling elephant tracks at 16,000 ft. He says his porters were terrified, believing the prints to be those of the **Abominable Snowman**.
■ England win the First Test at Brisbane by 322 runs. Australia collapse in their second innings and are all out for 58.

9 Wednesday

There is a meeting of the Cabinet at 7.30pm in the House of Commons. Walter Monckton, the King's legal adviser, visits Downing Street at midnight.
■ **Aston Villa** football team, due to play the Army at Aldershot, get lost in the fog and go

to the cinema in Reading instead.
■ A Royal Dutch Airlines **plane crashes** at Croydon. 14 are killed, among whom are Juan de la Cierva, inventor of the autogiro, and Admiral Arvid Lindmann, prime minister of Sweden 1928-30. There are three survivors.

10 Thursday

The King sends a message to the Houses of Parliament (and simultaneously to the Commonwealth governments) announcing his decision to abdicate in favour of his brother Albert, Duke of York, after a reign of just 325 days. Newsreels prepared in anticipation of the abdication are flashed on screens in cinemas and theatres minutes after Mr Baldwin's announcement in Parliament. In New York. the full text is broadcast direct from London, all other programmes being set aside. There is worldwide relief that the crisis is over. Crowds gather outside Buckingham Palace calling for the new King. (see panel, page 92)

11 Friday

Wildly cheering crowds engulf the Duke of York's car as he returns to 145 Piccadilly after seeing Queen Mary. King Edward loses his royal titles and it is thought he will leave the country tomorrow. The new King is to be known as **George VI**. The Dominions assent swiftly to the abdication. In France, *Le Matin* says, 'Mr Baldwin saved the monarchy, if not the monarch.'
■ For the second time in less than a year a new edition of the **Prayer Book** will be printed, and new postage stamps produced.
... Conductor John Barbirolli is appointed conductor of the New York Philharmonic Orchestra for a period of three years ...

KING WHO PUT LOVE

King cannot be allowed to harm the revered institution of the British Monarchy
– *Sydney Morning Herald*

King will do the wise thing and will not falter
– *Melbourne Age*

Allegiance to the Crown is the link that binds the Commonwealth. A rift would be calamitous
– *Toronto Evening Telegraph*

Constitutional crisis not confined to Britain alone. It is one wherein the whole of the Dominions is deeply concerned
– *Cape Times*

Every true Irishman will hope and pray that the King's decision will be dictated by wisdom rather than by sentiment. – *Irish Times*

THE BRITISH NEWSPAPERS, which have maintained a discreet silence for months, unlike their foreign counterparts, finally reveal the romance between the KING and Mrs WALLIS SIMPSON. Stanley Baldwin handles the crisis with great skill, supported by the leaders of the dominions, and their countries' press (above) But, after all alternatives have been explored, the King decides to abdicate. The crown passes to his brother the Duke of York, and King Edward VIII, now known as the Duke of Windsor, leaves his country in the middle of the night on the destroyer HMS *Fury*.

BEFORE THE THRONE

THE KING IN CRISIS: (clockwise from top left): letter of Abdication; the King and Mr Baldwin in coversation at the height of the crisis; The Duke and Duchess of Windsor after the abdication; the Duke of Windsor making his farewell broadcast, and in the car on his way to voluntary exile; the new King and Queen Elizabeth.

12 Saturday

It is announced that Prince Edward will address the nation at 10 o'clock tonight. Every radio set in London is bought or borrowed. The new King is proclaimed at 11 o'clock in Friary Court, St James's Palace by Garter King of Arms. The proclamation is then read, as tradition demands, at Charing Cross, 3.30pm; Temple Bar, 3.45pm and the Royal Exchange, 4.00pm. At his Accession Council, the King announces that he has conferred a dukedom on his brother who would henceforth be known as the Duke of Windsor. MPs take their oath of allegiance to the new King .

13 Sunday
New Moon.

The Duke of Windsor leaves the UK in the early hours of the morning aboard the destroyer HMS *Fury*, with a destroyer escort, and arrives at Boulogne at 3.55pm. He takes a train to Vienna, where he arrives at 10.15pm and motors to Enzefeld where he is to be the guest of Baron Edouard de Rothschild. Meanwhile, King George VI takes his daughters to morning service at Marlborough House. The Queen has a cold.

14 Monday

The King's birthday— he is 41. He confers the Order of the Garter on his wife, **Queen Elizabeth**. In Austria, the Duke of Windsor plays golf.
■ Bitter cold and heavy snow in **Spain.** Madrid enjoys a week of peace after four weeks of continuous shelling.
■ Potters are to make EIGHT MILLION new Coronation mugs and beakers. Stocks of **Edward VIII mugs** are exhausted.

15 Tuesday

General Franco has told the German government that he needs 60,000 more men to win the war in Spain.

■ More than 200 London streets have been given new names in 1936.
■ King George takes over all **racehorses** in training and at stud from his brother. His first runner will be *Marconi,* who is running tomorrow at Windsor.

16 Wednesday

London Zoo complains the the animals are lonely in December as hardly anyone comes to see them.
■ The Italians are smoking more cigarettes and cigars, and pipes are out of fashion. Tobacco is a state monopoly, and the gross takings in the past fiscal year amount to £34 million.
■ The King's horse *Marconi,* running for the first time in the new King's colours, finishes last but one at Windsor.

17 Thursday

The Pope (81), collapses. He is suffering from a combination of ailments including gout, a weak heart and asthma.
■ Two copies of *The Mint*, **Col T E Lawrence's** brilliant unpublished diary of his life in the RAF, are lodged at the Library of Congress in Washington, DC, USA, and two copies are offered for sale at £100,000 a copy. There is no prospect of publication in the UK for 25 years. Lawrence asked his brother not to publish while anyone mentioned in the text is still alive.

18 Friday

The start of the **Second Test** in Sydney, Australia. England win the toss and bat.
■ Large numbers of German troops, accompanied by the latest transport vehicles, continue to arrive in Spain. The total is believed to be 12,500.
■ The US Post Office is to transport 6,000 tons of gold bullion worth £12 billion from the Treasury vaults in Washington, DC, to the US government's new gold-storage facility at **Fort Knox**, Kentucky.

21 Monday

Australia collapse in the 1st innings of the Second Test in Sydney, scoring 67-7 after England declare at 426-6.

■ **Lord Nuffield** is giving £2 million to the Special Areas — S Wales, Durham, Tyneside, Cumberland and Scotland - to create employment and social improvements. The money will be administered by three trustees who will have total power to use it as they like. Lord Nuffield's gifts this year total £6,340,000.

■ Cunard White Star are bombarded with suggestions that their new liner No 552 should be called the *Queen Elizabeth*.

22 Tuesday

In the Second Test, Australia reach 208-3 in their 2nd innings but then collapse as England win. There are three more to play in the **Ashes** series.

■ The Post Office takes on 13,000 extra staff to deal with the **Christmas rush**. Mail posted daily in London is between 13-16 million units.

■ **Turkeys** are on sale at Smithfield Market, London, at 10d. per lb.

... **The Queen Mary docks at Southampton 13 hours late after fighting her way through mountainous seas.**

■ In the UK, Post Office staff protest through their union about the practice of sending game and poultry through the post with only a label around the neck. They would prefer it to be packed in boxes or baskets.

19 Saturday

In the Second Test at Sydney, England are 351 for 4 at lunch (Hammond 195 not out).

■ The start of two weeks' celebration in Holland leading up to the wedding of **Princess Juliana** of the Netherlands and Prince Bernhard,.

... **Trotsky and his wife leave Norway for Mexico, where they have been granted permission to live ...**

20 Sunday

A chemical substance, that when added to alcoholic drinks renders them innocuous, is patented in Germany.

■ The **Duke of Kent** celebrates his 34th birthday. It is announced that he will attend Princess Juliana's wedding.

23 Wednesday

Lord Nuffield's gift of £2 million for the 'special areas' is greeted with joy. Added to the government measures it means that the special areas will be able to turn the corner.

■ **Fog** covers the country. It is expected to last for three days.

24 Thursday
Christmas Eve

The Pope delivers his Christmas message from his bed. Within five minutes of him speaking, the address is broadcast in French, German, Polish and several other languages.

■ The Duke of Windsor's Christmas presents are delivered to Enzefeld by special courier.
■ In New York, **Sarah Churchill** says she and **Vic Oliver** will be married tomorrow morning and will honeymoon on board the *Aquitania*, which sails at noon.

25 Friday
Christmas Day.

The Duchess of Kent gives birth to a 7lbs daughter. Mother and child are doing well.
■ In London, there are a record number of **Christmas babies**. Queen Charlotte's (maternity) Hospital is so busy, with 15 births, that it has to close its doors.
■ A plump American turkey makes a misguided break for freedom at Whipsnade and lands in the Arctic Fox enclosure, providing them with an unexpected Christmas dinner.

26 Saturday
Boxing Day.

Charles Laughton and **Elsa Lanchester**, playing Captain Hook and Peter in *Peter Pan*, open to a somewhat mixed reception.
■ Britain is sending 10,000 **scouts** to the World Jamboree to be held next August in Amsterdam.

27 Sunday

The Archbishop of Canterbury broadcasts to the nation. He feels God is crowded out of modern life and deplores the drift from old standards.
■ The King, Queen and two princesses walk to Church at Sandringham. 6,000 people cheer them.
■ The Duke of Windsor issues a statement thanking the many hundreds of people who have written to him this Christmas and expressing his regret that he will not be able to answer them all personally.

28 Monday
Full Moon

■ Norwich Museum is given a cocked hat that belonged to **Admiral Nelson**. He had his portrait painted for Norwich in 1801 by Sir William Beechey. He gave Sir William the hat, which remained in the Beechey family until now.
■ The **Post Office** has had its busiest Christmas ever. In the two days before Christmas it handled 200 million letters and five million parcels.
■ **Jim Mollison** and Edouard Corniglion-Molinier, who failed in their last attempt to beat the record flight from England to Capetown, are to try again.
. . . TIM, the Speaking Clock, is two mins fast — the Post Office says it is a fault on the telephone line from Greenwich Observatory . . .

29 Tuesday

The government closes down the British embassy in Madrid, and moves it to Valencia.
■ **The Pope's** condition is grave.
■ The 70 islanders of Soay, an island off the coast of Skye, may petition the King for the evacuation of the island. A disastrous fishing season following a series of severe winters means that the islanders are existing in conditions of semi-starvation.
■ The demand for seats for the Coronation is greater than anticipated because of the presence of the Queen and the two princesses.

30 Wednesday

The BBC is to broadcast the wedding of Princess Juliana and Prince Bernhard in the Netherlands.
■ Famous French artist **Maurice Utrillo** (53), is suing the Tate Gallery for **libel.** They have listed him among the dead artists in the gallery's catalogue.The muddle occurred with a Spanish writer of the same name who died some years ago.

31 Thursday

A girl attending the **Chelsea Arts Ball** at the Royal Albert Hall is turned away by a commissionaire as he considered her costume of 'just a few autumn leaves' a bit daring.
■ In 1936, one person was killed or injured on Britain's roads every two minutess.
■ The Vatican say that **Pope Pius XI's** illness is slowly pursuing its fatal course.